My Wobl

Meditations on Cancer and the Creative Life

Published by Mission Point Press
2554 Chandler Lake Road, Traverse City, MI, 49696
MissionPointPress.com

ISBN: 978-1-943995-17-2
Library of Congress Control Number: 2016914847

Printed in the United States of America.

FLEDA BROWN

My Wobbly Bicycle

Meditations on Cancer
and the Creative Life

I pretty much functioned automatically, except to cry. Every once in a while I would think, "What do I eat? how do I act to announce or preserve my new status as temporary upon the earth?"

— *Audre Lorde, The Cancer Journals*

Just because we're going to die, doesn't mean we have to camp out in graveyards."

— *my favorite episode of NYPD Blue*

Table of Contents

Introduction

How does a writer deal with her cancer? By writing, of course. Week by week, I wrote and posted my thoughts and impressions, how I was wobbling along with my writing life, my griefs and a few joys. That's what you have here, a real-time account. Those who followed my blog at the time told me it helped them to understand, and those who had cancer, or who had someone close to them with cancer, told me it was like having a friend there with them. We were holding hands.

This book is a gift to the new Cowell Family Cancer Center in Traverse City, Michigan, where I live. The full amount of sales will go specifically to their Health & Wellness Suite. I'm glad we're beginning to act on the knowledge that body and mind are not separate. The immune system is more complex than we used to think, and can respond to a multiplicity of approaches.

The Health and Wellness Suite provides space for physical, emotional and spiritual healing for patients, staff, family members, caregivers and the community. There are rooms for touch therapy, such as Asian bodywork, acupuncture, Australian Bowen therapy and massage. There is an active yoga program, including restorative and healing classes developed for oncology patients. The Suite includes a meditation room with beautiful stained glass art representing the four seasons to provide a non-denominational space for quiet and meditation. Guided meditation classes, some with live music or art, are taught free of charge for the community. Wandering musicians play acoustic classical guitar through-out the Cancer Center, and there is a bi-monthly wellness speaking series featuring speakers from the community, as well as various workshops and retreats, and an anti-cancer book group that discusses texts having to do with health and wellness.

I hope this book helps you, or those you love who have cancer. We all need all the help we can get.

Fleda Brown

My Wobbly Bicycle

1   Learning to Ride

IT DOESN'T MATTER IF I repeat this a thousand times: "Socrates is a man. All men are mortal. Therefore Socrates is mortal." All these years my mind has maneuvered around this roadblock. I am wondering how to say this. I am thinking that matters of life and death are to be approached with reverence, even when we turn the reverence awkwardly into a joke. When it's our own life that's in danger, it seems arrogant to freight it with grand importance; it seems trivializing not to; it seems negligent not to talk about it. I found out three weeks ago that I have endometrial cancer. I had surgery on Thursday, a complete hysterectomy. The surgeon says the muscle of the uterus was "deeply penetrated" with the cancer.

I don't yet know what this means. I'll have test results next week.

Where am I now? Thrown summarily over to the side of those who know they'll die. On the other hand, life goes on: get out of bed, fix oatmeal, get on with it. I feel, though, strangely as if I've been in training for this moment for more than twenty-five years. I've spent so many hours on my meditation cushion, gone to so many retreats. There must be help in that. I suppose my old solid self doesn't feel so solid any more. Not so much a "thing" to "lose." I can't say. I have no answers to anything and certainly don't expect profundity to show up just because I'm in danger.

I'm 68. I've had two children, two D & C's, a tubal ligation and a couple of foot surgeries—in other words, I've been under the knife before. I've looked into the bright lights as I was wheeled into the OR with perfect confidence. All will be well. This time, I have to say, I was scared. The polished floors, the glare of lights, and in the corner, the large, ominously hooded DaVinci machine that would extract the parts of my body I've used for all these years.

An amazing machine, the DaVinci robot. It poked five little holes in my belly, cut through and cauterized the arteries and ducts that connected my reproductive organs, so they could be pulled out the bottom. It even did the stitching, inside my body. The arms and fingers of the device are so delicate (and the screen the surgeon sits in front of magnifies so much) that it can peel a grape.

I have been home now a day and a half, and my stomach feels like someone punched me, but other than that, I'm fine. I may be in a little danger; I may be in a lot. I'll know next week. What I know for sure is that I'm surrounded by generosity. One small example: a couple of weeks ago, on top of this other news, I found I had a detached retina. I had surgery in the retinal surgeon's office. My husband Jerry said he'd leave his meeting and come pick me up, but nooooo, I said I could drive home okay. It wasn't far. I had one eye taped shut, the other blurry. Stupid. By the time I got home, I was trembling with fear and pain. But there was a big box waiting for me, containing a prayer shawl from my Episcopal friends in Delaware, each stitch accompanied by a prayer. I stood in the middle of the kitchen wrapped in the shawl, sobbing and damn happy. Prayers are prayers. I'll take what I can get. To me they sound like: "I've turned my attention to you right now. I wish the best for you. I love you."

We've had food arrive on our doorstep every day. Along with multiple offers to help with anything. And we've only lived in Traverse City six years now, retired from the east coast. Partly it was all that crystal-clear water, Grand Traverse Bay. But when we turned off down a tree-lined brick street, this is real life, is what I thought. Now that's silly. Maybe it's memories of my grandparents' houses in Missouri, that Craftsman architecture, those slightly cracked sidewalks, big trees. I don't know. I felt anchored, the possibility of anchoring. I'm a romantic.

So, here we are, cozily tucked into the middle of the country, surrounded by people who've become dear to us. Now everything's shifted. We pretend there's some solidity, some predictability. But being alive is more like riding a bicycle, balancing on two thin tires. Eventually we'll fall one way or the other, but for the moment, we're upright. It's exciting, sometimes frightening. I remember learning to ride, my father holding me on a grown-up bike, wooden blocks on the pedals so I could reach them. The fear of handling something too big for me.

2   The Lights Flicker

I WRITE POEMS, FOR the most part. In poems I generally slow down language —with line-breaks, with dazzle and play, lyricism and ponderousness—so that there can be some staying-with-the-moment: being there. So what now, when the ultimate slowing down is a real possibility? I want prose. I'm flat-footed, going from one thing to the next.

I wish I could tell you what it was like, to hear the news. Much worse than we'd expected. When I noticed what I knew was a tell-tale sign a couple of months ago, my doctor examined me and said, "Well, I don't feel anything there, but we might send you for an ultrasound, anyway." The ultrasound showed what looked like a small cyst. My doctor sent me to a gynecologist, who said, "Let's do a D & C. I think if we just clean you out, you'll be fine." No worries. The Monday morning after the D & C, the gynecologist called, asked how I felt, and chatted calmly for a few minutes. Or hours. Then he said, "I'm surprised, I didn't expect this at all, but the tissue samples show cancer."

If I knew how to say what came next. The lights flicker. The mind, the heart, the body, each run off into their separate corners. Not speaking to each other. The mind registering the fact. The heart metaphorically stopping, the body, I'd say, numbing itself. That's as close as I can come. As fate would have it, Jerry was just on his way out the door to the dentist when I yelled at him to come upstairs. "I have cancer," I said. We sat on the edge of the bed repeating this so-called fact to each other. "Go on," I said. "Do your teeth. Let me soak this in while you're gone."

While he was gone, I paced. Tried to work the information down into me. "I'm sure we'll just have the hysterectomy and I'll be fine," I told the kids on the phone, and believed it.

Now, what I'm doing is gathering information, deciding between joining a clinical trial group or not (decided not), getting a CAT scan, looking online at wigs and caps, preparing for my three-to-four month blast of chemo and radiation, the vicious murder of all fast-growing cells in my body. In battle-mode, people say. She's "fought" her cancer. After a long "battle" with cancer, he succumbed. Apparently this language for cancer emerged during the first of the serious cancer drug research, during World War II. Battle seemed natural. Earlier in our history, there was little hope in "fighting" illness. God, or Fate, saved you or not. How fiercely we want to survive. Of course we do. I do. The cancer is in my lymph nodes. Stage 3C-2. In case you haven't had to learn this, there are only four stages possible and only three substages: A,B, and C. The last number is 2 out of 3. I'm perched on the edge of the worst.

My local writing group gave me a light-sword for a present! I love it that they want to fight the universe with me. I am in complete sympathy with Thomas Hardy's wish for a vengeful God to shake a fist at, rather than the "purblind Doomsters" who "had as readily strown / Blisses about my pilgrimage as pain."

I think, though, of the effect of battle-language. As we now know, nothing gets thrown "away." There is no "away" to throw things to. No enemy gets "destroyed." There's always an opposite force mounting itself in response. What gets pushed away springs back like a rubber-band. So, what language for this trouble I'm in? This is what I've come up with:

> You can pave over the grass, but if there's the tiniest crack anywhere, a pale little blade will soon emerge. Life is deter-mined to live. Life, of course, is not just the growing and developing part. The sprig that emerges is going to die when it's finished with the other, as part of the wholeness of things.

It could be that I'm finished with the other. It feels as if I'm not. There's a great deal of life going on in me. I have a lot of work I want to do. My stand-up paddleboard is waiting for me next summer. My children and grandchildren are waiting for all of us to be together at the lake again.

So, as I head into chemo, my intention is to stay curious. I'm a Buddhist—well, I've never felt called to take the precepts, or vows, but I've been practicing all these years. The whole idea of practice is just that: curiosity. Just observe. No, really look. Really. See how we're not separate from anything. Everything is attached to everything. Where is life going? Where is it now? It's in this computer keyboard, in the poem I want to get back to, in my awareness of my husband downstairs answering emails, in the tick of his mother's ancient clock, in the warmth of my green tea. A LOT of green tea! Have you seen the statistics on how much good it does?

I don't know how to say any of this. The truth always eludes me, as soon as I think I've found a clever phrase to pin it down. I don't know why I bother. But it does seem that humans keep bothering. Well, you know, I'm a poet. The bothering often seems more successful in poetry than in prose. Poems know how to point toward rather than to try to articulate the truth. Poems are written—the good ones—by people who stumble in the dark, feeling their way. I'm stumbling, or as I put it before, riding a wobbly bicycle. But I'm okay with wobbliness. Wobbliness focuses one amazingly, to stay upright. I'm sure the bicycle *wants* to stay upright, since it is so much fun to ride. I'm going to go with that.

3 Learn by Going

WHAT A DIFFERENCE ONE phone call makes! My CAT scan is normal. No additional tumors that the surgery missed. Still, there's chemo ahead of me. But. I've been anxious. And gloomy. With each of those previous tests, as I said, I'd been a bit nonchalant, since I felt fine. I've always been so healthy, yet each time the results have been so much worse than I imagined. Here I am, John Keats: "When I have fears that I may cease to be/ before my pen has gleaned my teeming brain. . . ." I especially know his mood at the end of the poem: "then on the shore / Of the wide world I stand alone, and think, / Till Love and Fame to nothingness do sink."

I've stared into space, feeling alone, even with all the love and friends. I have also thought—okay, I'm a literary sort of person— of D. H. Lawrence's short story, "Odor of Chrysanthemums," in which the widow and others scrub the dead body of her husband and she's struck by the utter otherness, the solitariness that's always been there.

Both my children came to spend last weekend with us, Kelly from D.C. and Scott from New Jersey! Kelly comes, as always, fired up, ready to do what needs doing. She has four children— the oldest now in college, the youngest in fifth grade. For the last 20 years, she's ferried children from one lesson to the next, and from soccer to baseball, or sport du jour. We look a lot alike: thin, delicate features, alert, ready for what might go wrong. To give you an example: when we (meaning the children, their step-father Dennis, and me) made the move from Arkansas to Delaware in 1978, we had a Ryder truck and our little car, one following the other. It was Kelly, alone, who kept us from ending up in Vermont, or Indiana. She read the map right, she spotted the turns. Anxious, yes. She comes by it honestly. She was ten when I married Dennis and our lives flew out from under us like a rug. She's been a runner for years, which burns off a lot of anxiety. She's a psychotherapist, which is no surprise. She worked her way out from under the burden of her childhood the same way I did, by trying to figure it out. Trying to work it out. She loves being with people. She loves movement. She was always out the door, with her friends. At night when I read to her and Scott, Scott would sit there forever. She was jumping up before the story was over.

Scott, on the other hand, is the geeky one. He read in the near-dark in his room—*The Phantom Tollbooth, Where the Red Fern Grows* (he cried at the end), Piers Anthony Xanth books, *Dr. Who* (he had a huge collection), heaps of other science-fiction books. And comics, surrounded by stuffed animals and Pink Floyd posters. He built glorious and complicated Lego cities before there were fancy parts that did half the work for you. He latched onto Pac-Man as soon as it was invented. He rescued me from my panic and desperation when the University insisted all faculty buy and learn to use computers. Scott's now a Chief Architect at IBM. I suppose this was his natural inclination, but on the other hand, when he was four, his father was replaced by an unpredictable and volatile step-father. Best hang out in your own room and burrow down into small, manageable things—pixels, words. He survived, sometimes had a good laugh with Dennis, and he sometimes felt, as Kelly did, tenderness for that suffering, erratic permanent visitor in their home.

I'm continually grateful that they love me, after all I've put them through. I've spent a good part of my life stumbling, trying to shake loose the shackles of a—what?—"deeply troubled" childhood? That cliché's as good as any other. In any case, I've gotten myself in big trouble by not being able to see the nose in front of my face.

I married Harry, their father, when I was 17, still in high school. I wasn't pregnant, only lonely and confused. But I was an excellent student, responsible as hell, and headed straight for college after that. I needed that marriage. I needed someone, it hardly mattered who, to put his arm around me. The man who happened to show up was a junior in civil engineering at the University of Arkansas. What was he doing, dating a high school student? He was a loner, a bit brooding, with migraines, a decent student, reliable. Then I started growing up. And away. Speaking of deceptively solid ground, for maybe eight of the twelve years we were married, I was doggedly working to create the illusion—to myself and every-one else—that there was solid ground under what was less and less a marriage. That I wasn't growing daily more miserable. Then his drinking escalated. I thought it was my fault.

Less than two years after the divorce, I married Dennis in a quick fit of rapture. I was teaching high school and taking a graduate semi-nar at night. He was a star graduate student writing his dissertation on D. H. Lawrence, invited to our class to speak. He was wearing a light blue knit short-sleeve shirt. I remember watching the perfect hairs on his perfectly slim arm as he talked. Something about that. So confident, so, well, spiritual, so different from the bour-bon-scented engineer who picked the children up on weekends. You would think, from listening to him, that he was Lawrence reincarnated. Kelly was eleven, Scott seven. I should have known better. On our second date, he passionately locked his Laurentian brown eyes onto mine and asked me to marry him. How can I explain this other than as a resolute romantic plunge into disaster? Even his mother was worried sick that he was marrying a woman with "those two precious babies."

He finished his Ph.D. at the University of Arkansas and got hired at the University of Delaware. I finished my coursework toward my Ph.D. (I came back the following summer for exams), we packed everything into a Ryder truck and Leroy and headed north, leav-ing my beloved home, my children's beloved home, behind, into territory we barely imagined. My life was driven; I was not the driver of it. Off the edge of a cliff, as they say.

Nonetheless, here we are now in Michigan—the three of us at the moment, plus Jerry, my beloved husband of 21 years now. We're watching TV; the news is the Sandy Hook School murders. I'm glad to have this "normal" time with them before I begin chemo. We sit around the table watching the memorial service, all of us tearing up or crying. Kelly says she thinks she couldn't endure that, as a mother, unless she had a thought of some life after death, of something continuing. Scott, who has two children, said no, those thoughts diminish the preciousness of the life we have. This is what we have, and it's up to us to use it the best we can.

I see this from a Buddhist perspective, of course, which is not so easily explained. What is that "thing" Freud called the Ego, the "self"? We convince ourselves that we live within the small idea of it. If we didn't, good heavens, would we exist? But it's a fiction. It can't be found. What's real is spacious, and interconnected with everything else. You could say it that way. Our bodies die, but we don't die in the sense that what we thought was "us" didn't exist in the first place. Does all this comfort me? Yes, a little.

I think of St. Teresa of Avila, St. John of the Cross, Hildegard of Bingen, the Buddha. And Jesus, of course. I can see them all looking into the vastness that has no name, that has no "religion," that is just what it is, the great "I Am." They called it perfect, complete. They lived in both worlds, the provisional one that has beginnings and endings and toothaches and squabbles and the other, absolute one. And both of them are the same thing. And not. My head is spinning. Yours, probably, too! I cannot think myself out of trouble. No one can, apparently.

Back here in the mundane world, Jerry got the snow-blower started at last, in time for the big snow coming. The doctor called to say his hemoglobin count—which we'd been worried about—is, after all, normal. I may get to start chemo before Christmas. As I said, things are looking up.

4   Hat in Hand

DECEMBER 26 AND COASTING. My "planning" appointment with the surgeon is Jan. 3. I suppose we'll start chemo soon after that. Meanwhile, my poor body is recovering from the sudden extraction of its heretofore valuable parts. I still want a nap in the afternoons, but I can walk or stay on the treadmill for thirty minutes, no problem.

Why oh why? Me. Can't help but let that surface now and then. Susan Sontag, in her book, *Illness as Metaphor,* railed against the "blame the victim" idea that our illnesses "fit" our psychology, that our repressions make themselves known in the body in appropriate areas. She insisted that it's all straight physiology, nothing to do with our minds. It does seem natural for us to want to find reasons. If we didn't look for reasons, we would have no effective drugs, no science at all. But since reasons are found by looking at select blocks of information, it isn't possible to see everything at once as it's all interacting. Heisenberg's Uncertainty Principle shows that as soon as we think we've "found" something, we've skewed the evidence.

My D.O. says that as we age, cells just mutate now and then. It's pretty much random, he seemed to say. My chiropractor says— although he wouldn't go so far as to claim it caused my cancer—I have a lot of "old" holding in my spine, nothing recent. I can look back: there's all that stress, all my life. But the last 20 years have been pretty wonderful. I've done some *serious* psychotherapy: I don't think I'm "repressed." I've had this steady and dedicated meditation practice all these years. I'm a poster child of eating well and living well. Maybe it's true that the past was storing itself up, waiting to explode.

I will never know, any more than I will know why I have an allergy to leaf mold. I'm a conglomeration of causes and conditions from the near- and long-past, as well as the present.

I can't see this cancer, I can't smell it or taste it. I have no symptoms. I only know it's there because machines have told my doctors this is the case. It may be all gone, along with my various organs, but it's doubtful, since it was found in the lymph nodes. Likely there are stray cells waiting to bloom and spread if they aren't nuked. Actually, the cells are like most other things. I can't see any of the x's and o's that turn my tapping into words on the page. I can't see germs or love or oxygen or gravity or the choral music I'm listening to, or what my face looks like to others.

Ted Kooser, our former U.S. poet laureate, is one of my touchstones for weathering the storm. He wrote to me, "When my doctor told me that cancer had spread to the lymph nodes.... He said, 'You are about to enter one of the great life-affirming experiences,' and he was right. You'll come through your chemo more in love with life than you can even imagine right now."

Okay, Ted.

Ted wrote a series of poems as post cards to Jim Harrison while Ted was recovering from his chemo. Here's one poem I feel as if I'm writing, myself, at the moment.

Feb 21 Sunny and Clear

Fate, here I stand, hat in hand,
in my fifty-ninth year,
a man of able body and a merry spirit.
I'll take whatever work you have.

5   I Loved Being Sick

I'M LEANING MY WOBBLY bike against a tree for now, since I won't see the doctor until tomorrow. I'll report later on what I learn. In the meantime—you'll see this is relevant—I want to tell you about my book that's just out, co-written with Sydney Lea, called *Growing Old in Poetry: Two Poets, Two Lives,* from Autumn House Press. Syd and I share being poet laureate of our respective states. I'm former poet laureate of Delaware; Syd is the current poet laureate of Vermont. We had the idea that if we picked topics and each headed out as we wished with that topic, we could cover a lot of territory, both artistic and memoirish. But it's this one essay, "Staying Home From School," that seems relevant to the situation. How ironic it is to me, now. I wrote this no more than six months ago. Our topic was illness. I want to quote this for you. It may be a small window into the present:

> I loved being sick. If my body couldn't work up the germs, my mind could. Through grade school, all the way through high school, I was deft at turning a slightly scratchy throat into a wicked possible strep condition that would keep me home from school. To cinch the matter, I would vigorously rub the thermometer, or hold it under warm water at the bathroom sink when no one was looking, I don't know if my mother bought any of this, or if she was just too harried and/ or depressed to fight me on it.

The half-year my aunt Cleone and her three wildly healthy boys lived with us in Columbia, I would be "sick" and my Aunt Cleone would position herself at my bedroom door, frowning. "Fleda, are you *really* sick enough to stay home?" she'd ask. She was onto me, which almost spoiled my day, but not quite.

Our house, in truth, was a house of illness. My brother was severely mentally retarded and had grand mal seizures so awful that each one would take your breath away. There was a heap of bottles, all full of potent drugs, on the kitchen counter, along with an apothecary's mortar and pestle to grind up the ones too difficult for him to swallow. My mother developed severe arthritis—no wonder. My father had only allergies, but he was able to make a great deal out of lying on his back on the bed with his head over the side, dripping Neo-Synephrine into a stuffed-up nose. Don't get me wrong—we were also very physical. My mother loved to walk, arthritis or no. She could move really fast, her scarf tied under her chin like a Russian peasant; my father rode his bike several miles to school when almost no one did such a thing; my sister and I rode bikes, swam, played rudimentary tennis, and walked. But it appears to me now that the one way I could be assured that my parents' attention would be directed at me was to be sick.

And also, I was shy —I guess you could call it that. In any case, I found being at home, being taken care of, very comforting. My mother would have liked to be a nurse and seemed to enjoy having me home, bringing me poached egg on toast, straightening my covers, finding the paper-doll pages in McCall's magazine for me, bringing me scissors and Scotch tape. The kid in Robert Louis Stevenson's "The Land of Counterpane" was me:

When I was sick and lay a-bed,
I had two pillows at my head,

And all my toys beside me lay,
To keep me happy all the day.

In fact, I remember lying there reading *A Child's Garden of Verses*. They were too young for me, but I loved them anyway. School was always pressure—get the math problems right, do well on the test, and carefully manage to fit into certain groups of friends. I think I was a bit afraid of people. Being alone felt safer, easier. . . . in the mornings when my father was at school, teaching, and my mother was puttering around, taking care of Mark and washing clothes, the house was quiet, peaceful—her little radio in the kitchen tuned to the Arthur Godfrey show or whatever followed that.

Before publication, I added a postscript: "If I follow the lines of this essay, would I have to say that I brought this cancer on? Not on your life. I have a good life, and work that I'm eager to continue. I don't want to stay home from school anymore."

6   Wally the Buddha Cat

AT THE END OF the hall in my oncologist's
suite of offices is a large room with a fireplace and soft music piped in. Winter sun is
pouring in the huge windows and flashing
off the metal poles and trays for the chemo
drips. There are five plush leather reclin-
ers, each with its pole on wheels next to it,
so you can drag it along with you if you need to go to the restroom.
There's a water cooler, a small refrigerator, and a basket of snacks.
We're three blocks from Grand Traverse Bay, which was gorgeous
in the morning sun when Jerry and I drove here. The oncologist is
actually only a few blocks from our house. Under other conditions,
I would have walked. I can also walk to the hospital if I want, for
blood tests. Praise be for small towns that have what you need in
them.

The nurse starts the anti-nausea drug and Benadryl (to ward off
any possible allergic reactions) at about 10:00. This makes me
dopey and a bit incoherent. They drip in for a half hour before
she starts the Taxol (wicked name). Jerry comes back and brings
us sandwiches at noon. About 1:00, she starts the (equally wicked)
Carboplatin. She is always just a few steps away, monitoring me,
taking my blood pressure. We're done by 2:00.

It comes to me at some point in my fog how deeply my spirit is
affected by this. I've walked, ridden my bike, swum, eaten carefully and well. I have, as they say, "taken care of myself." I'll
continue to do what I can, but now comes this time when I have

to let these terrible chemicals nigh unto kill me, monitored so they come right to the edge of killing me. I'm thinking that this is the very definition of the spiritual: surrendering (it's a kind of dying)—not aimlessly— but surrendering to the specific accumulated wisdom-teachings of whatever calls to us: our religion, medicine, both, whatever's needed at the time. We follow the teachings, not always understanding why, sometimes not even approving of them with our rational mind, bringing as much trust to the situation as we can.

I've only been able to drag a very few feeble poems out of me lately, yet I'm writing this remembrance in my head if I can't sleep, and at odd times during the day. I consult Wally the Buddha cat (a stray miracle of joy who's come to us in our time of need) for his take on this. Verily, he sayeth unto me: when the food dish is being filled, there is no thinking about which way to turn. One turns toward the food and prosaically eats. But when one tosses the toy mouse into the air with one paw, one turns one's back and acts as if one could care less about it, this is poetry. It requires a gap, a once-removal from the thing-wanted. A playing, if you will, with the language of hunger. Ah, yes. Gassho, Wally.

7   Type a Little Faster

So, A GROUP OF scientists sit around trying to figure what might yield the greatest results in demonstrating to basically oblivious humans what being "Alive" means. Or, well, maybe they're celestial scientists, from one realm or the other. After much discussion, they arrive at: *chemotherapy.*

I was doing so well. Chemo on Tuesday, Wednesday feeling good; Thursday I took a long walk on the beach. "I'm doing great," I told my friends, in my steroidal enthusiasm. By Thursday night, the body started registering the assault upon its integrity. Sleepless night. Friday much worse.

Saturday, oh, oh, oh.

Like the flu, you could say, but that isn't it. Aching, yes. Unable to think about eating anything except cream of wheat, baked potato, chicken noodle soup. Not wanting even to drink the required amount of water. Sounds like the flu, but there's a quality to it that I can only describe as deathly. A sourly metallic taste to it. The body knows it's been poisoned. You can feel the bone marrow beginning to suffer. Body and mind, in perfect concert, grow horrified. And this is only the first whammy. I'm told to expect each cycle of chemo to register deeper, last longer, killing as it goes.

Sunday night I started to feel better enough to let down and have a good, long cry. Have I said I've cried? Not much. Clear-headedness has saved my soul, over and over. Did I cry when my brother Mark had a terrible seizure? No, I reached for a towel to support his head. Did I cry when my mother was sobbing and my father was yelling? No, I got angry. Why was she so weak? Did I cry when I asked Harry to move out? Oh yes, oh yes, but before that, and in front of the children, stoicism. Did I cry when I left Dennis? Buckets. But by then I was in therapy and learning how to do that. I did, after all, love him, but when someone can't be fixed, and when life is intolerable, you buck up, get tough and leave. And then cry, buckets. Alone.

Now, when I can, when something relaxes enough to allow it, the tears come from the center of the earth, from my heart, my body, everything so sad, so sad at the thought of losing all this, this life I love. Not bitter, just sad. Not angry at the gods, just sad.

It's Monday morning. Apparently the toxins have worked their way through. My body wakes up with life starting to flood through me. Not "again"—but as if I'd never felt it. As if I'd never felt what it is to live—to be physically alive—before. The outline of existence painting itself in luminous colors. Intangible but palpable.

We have to continually be jumping off cliffs and developing our wings on the way down. —Ray Bradbury

I'll have 3 cycles of chemo, followed by 5 weeks of daily targeted radiation, then three more cycles of chemo. A long road, into June. But now I've seen how it goes. I may forget that I'll come back from each one, but Jerry can remind me. Meanwhile, here I am, doubling up on all this, writing it down as if the whole contained a hole, and my assignment were to fill in with words.

If my doctor told me I had only six minutes to live, I wouldn't brood. I'd type a little faster. —Isaac Asimov.

8   Flashing Eyes, Floating Hair

I NEED A SHOWER, so I put a nylon squeegee over the drain to catch hair. Oh, there's quite a lot. When I get out, towel my head carefully and run mousse through, large soggy heaps come out in my hands. I call Jerry. We agree. I take the scissors and cut the front as short as I can. Jerry cuts the back. No one is crying, no one is laughing. We're doing a job here. My head emerges. The lines of my fontanels, visible for the first time since infancy.

What is all this about hair? And teeth, I think, are the same. Aren't we all drawn to life, blowing full in the breeze (Coleridge: "His flashing eyes, his floating hair!") or chomping down on prey, asserting aliveness. I look at myself in the mirror. Well, nice head shape, I think. And too, how strange to see what for most women, at least, is hidden all our lives.

The shaved head! In the Middle Ages, denuding a woman of what was supposedly her most seductive feature was the typical punishment for adultery. In 1923, German women who were accused of having relations with the French were humiliated by having their heads shaved. And during WW II, the Nazis ordered German women accused of sleeping with non-Aryans to be publicly punished the same way.

Prisoners often have their heads shaved, supposedly to stop the spread of lice, but also, of course, it's demeaning. But Buddhist monks have their heads shaved, too—a sign of their commitment to the Holy Life, of one gone forth into unrootedness.

I know a beautiful woman who has alopecia, I think. She shaves her head. She's as regal as Sinead O'Conner. I think also of many African American women who cut their hair as short as Obama's, how lovely their heads often look, how much emphasis that puts on the neck, the eyes, the mouth. Beauty's a matter of perception, highly influenced by genetic predisposition, I think.

Yet, I've spent all these years looking at myself with hair. I love hair. It changes like the wind, one day perfect, the next flyaway wretched, but still, it touches the neck, it frames the face. I have (had) nice hair. It has some body and although fine, is (was) still thick. I am surprised that I'm not more alarmed at the moment at having no hair. I may be in shock. I have cancer.

Before my hair fell out, Jerry and my hairdresser Jessica went with me to "Crowning Glory," the wig store. Ironic? You could read it that way. Many women look beautiful with scarves and hats. I think sometimes I'll want to wear hats in the house, but for me, looking in the mirror and seeing the same head I've always seen will be, I'm sure, a great morale booster. Also, I want people to look at me and see the same person. Am I in denial? Everyone who knows me knows I have cancer. But I think wearing hair will allow me to move among strangers without having them more internally focused on "Oh, that poor woman," and more on what we're talking about.

I spent some time deciding who I should be. Perky? Vampy? Blonde? I settled on the person I'm used to. I sent my daughter a picture. She said she'd been trying to get me to get my hair cut like that. So when I have hair again, shall I tell Jessica to cut it like my wig?

Next, the eyebrows and lashes will go. They're already thinner.

9   Soup, Bread, Hats, and Scarves

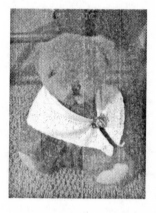

LAST TUESDAY'S CHEMO (#2) took a while to get to me. On Saturday, when the three days of steroids and anti-nausea pills were over, my wobbly bicycle got wobblier. Fatigue and achiness. White blood count dropped; I've been given an injection of Neulasta to get the bone marrow cranked up to produce more white blood cells. Which makes my bones ache.

Lying awake, I was pondering again this compulsion to say exactly what this is like, what anything is like. I was seeing the intersection of writer and reader, not as an intersection, but as a singularity. Not separate. We're carbon-based beings, entirely intertwined. We exist only in relation. Try to imagine anything existing without having to describe it in relation to something else. It feels as if my effort to talk about this is not so much me talking to you, but this particular area of existence worrying its way toward articulation, which is really all of us, straining toward awareness.

Why oh why do I lie awake trying to find exactly the right word? I am sure it's because the closer I get to what I know of my experience but can't quite say, the closer I am to the truth we share, but also can't be said. The right word is an opening, a gift.

Oh my, the gifts! I'm so grateful—all these friends and former students who've kept track of me. I've been teaching in the low-residency MFA program, the Rainier Writing Workshop in

Tacoma, Washington, for eight years. I taught at the University of Delaware for 27 years, and I was poet laureate of the state for seven years before we moved. All these lives are converging in my mail-box, my e-mail box.

Here come soup, bread, hats, hand-woven scarf, rosary, prayer shawls, teddy bear with an antique handkerchief for a shawl, paddle-boarding T-shirt, body lotion, more soup, more bread, special rock, eagle pin, trumpeter swan feathers, chocolate, cook-ies, notes, cards, hilarious Wonder Gifts (google-eyes, stick-on tattoos), chili, wool socks, hand-made jacket, yellow-submarine tea strainer, children's drawings, books, movies, an 11-CD set of *Lolita*, flowers, more flowers, baskets of "survival items" from crackers to lotions. How am I to take this all in?

At my last exam, my oncologist said I seemed a bit down (how good of him to notice). I said I'd just gotten four gifts in one day and was overwhelmed. Was I really "down?" That wasn't the right word, although I'd cried when the gifts arrived. I'd say I was feel-ing utterly vulnerable, needing to let a lot more of our common human affection touch me than I've had experience doing. It's hard to be vulnerable. It takes guts. At least for me.

As for writing, it seems to me that the entire endeavor to say what we mean requires a huge vulnerability. We arrive at a word that crosses the (imaginary) boundary between us all, and we're star-ing straight into the face of our own selves. That's where the guts come in. It's not an "other," it's us. As Gerard Manley Hopkins's speaker says to Margaret ("Spring and Fall") who's crying over the falling leaves:

Now no matter, child, the name:
Sorrow's springs are the same.
Nor mouth had, no nor mind, expressed
What héart héard of, ghóst guéssed:
It is the blight man was born for,
It is Margaret you mourn for.

10 Cosmic Timing

EVERY WEEK AN ADVENTURE. Monday I met with the radiation team to get "mapped" for radiation, which starts a week after my next chemo. Either I still haven't gotten used to living in the Midwest, or hospital staff everywhere are preternaturally sweet. The nurse in charge hugs me. The vile dye mixture I have to drink goes down with her tender solicitations. Another dye is intravenous.

Then I'm on the CT bed, my feet held slightly apart with a piece of foam and rubber banded together so they won't move. I'm lying on a mat that, when deflated, holds my midsection in position. My hands grip two handles above my head. For sure, I'm locked down. I get two CT scans, one before the intravenous dye and one after. Then I'm tattooed (permanently) with three tiny dots to line up the machines each time for radiation. More than you wanted to know? More than I wanted to know, too, but now that I'm in it, I am curious.

Wally does not know I'm sick. He lies across the back of the chair, a hairy white and gray decorative throw, or sits his heavy self in my lap to be rubbed. He knows about as much about what's going on with me as I do. Neither of us can see any evidence of illness. I do what I'm told because of the test tubes, CTs, and slides. Wally does what he's told, more or less, because Jerry and I are the keepers of the sacred *Iams* bag. He is a great comfort to me—he lives his life with seeming perfect aplomb within the confines allotted to him. He must stay inside, but what does "inside" mean, when there is only a picture of outside, out the window? Who knows if it (outside) exists or not? It is enough to watch it go by, like thoughts.

Wally plays with his food. He lies flat on the floor and scoops one morsel of food from his bowl at a time. He scoots it a little distance so it's necessary to capture it. He lies with his considerable ruff leaning in his water bowl. He takes a sip, looks away as if he is content never to drink again, then turns to take another sip. He is in possession of his life. He has perfect cosmic timing.

Wally came to us, limping and not wanting to take more than a few steps before he sat down. We checked everything and determined he had arthritis. After only a few days of a potent glucosamine mixture, he started leaping and chasing his mouse. Did he question any of that improvement? "What improvement?" he might ask. "One day I was one way, now I'm another. So?"

Humans get sick. We get well. We don't, or can't, look back much. We have a baby—we say we remember the pain, but we don't really. We have another, and when we're in labor again, we say, "Oh yes, this is what it's like. Now I remember." Same with grief, or love. We have the words, the thoughts, the muscle responses to the thoughts of the experience but we can't keep the experience. We only had it when we had it.

I'm having this cancer when I'm having it. I am in the middle of this, in my fuzzy hat, fuzzy socks, scarf with personally inscribed poems, red prayer shawl. In full regalia.

11   Acts of Awareness

THIRD CHEMO YESTERDAY. MY oncologist was a bit late for our appointment (There's always a pre-chemo exam). He'd been at the hospital and was obviously frustrated after talking with a patient. He didn't give particulars, but said something like this: heart disease is the #1 killer, cancer is #2. Even though heart disease has as many variables and is as much a mystery, somehow people assume the doctor is working in their best interest with heart disease, that a stent, certain medications, are appropriate. Yet with cancer, everyone has a different tangent, an anecdotal cure, they think may be better than what the doctor has in mind. Not that he discourages supplements, herbals, acupuncture, etc., but it's the attitude I could tell he was responding to.

It does seem that cancer feels more out-of-control to us. Meditation intends to make it quite clear to me that I am "out of control" in an ultimate sense. I can't dictate when I'll be born or die. About all I can do in this lifetime is encourage certain attitudes that can help lean me in a direction I want to go.

This chemo doesn't seem to be giving me much of a grace period of feeling good before the ickys set in. And here it is, full winter. I'm glad to have chemo and radiation this time of year. Caps and wigs make you hot. And I can wear a stocking cap now and feel like my old self when I go outside. But the dark and enclosure sometimes get to me, no matter how diligently I follow my cheering up routines. I am not all light sabre and optimism. Sometimes I sink. Sometimes, with Keats, "On the shore / of the wide world I stand alone, and think."

But there are books. I would like to sing the praises of novels and memoirs. My friend Janet lent me *The End of Your Life Book Club* by Will Schwalbe, a publisher with a distinguished career from a prominent family of publishers and philanthropists. He chronicles the last couple of years of his mother's life as she's dying of pancreatic cancer. They're both huge readers, and they talk their way through a pile of books during this time. You'd think I'd want a more cheerful book. But it did cheer me.

Will's mother, Mary Ann Schwalbe says, "When you walk around New York, or really anywhere, you see so many people like that young woman [in the book they're reading]—not desperate, but still sad and lonely. That's one of the amazing things great books like this do—they don't just get you to see the world differently, they get you to look at people, the people all around you, differently."

Great books, not schlock (although some schlock may be insightful, too). I'm not thinking of books-as-moral-lessons, either. I'm thinking of people's made-up or true stories as "acts of awareness," as D. H. Lawrence said. Hawthorne reminded us that the "truth of the human heart" is sometimes easier to see in what he called "romance" than it is right in front of our noses. We make up our lives in our minds whether we write them down or not. We are as mysterious as cancer. A book takes me deeply inside many minds, helps me see the close details of another life, which in a real sense is my own life.

My friend Nancy lent me *Shantaram*, by Gregory David Roberts, a huge thick book, a fictionalized account of the author's escape from an Australian prison. He ends up in Bombay, serving as a beloved doctor in the most horrible slums. He's thrown into a ghastly Indian jail, gets out, goes to Afghanistan to fight the Russians—it's epic in proportion. I liked holding the book Nancy bought in India: cheap paper, sometimes the print slanted on the page, bleeding through or too light.

I'm now reading *The Emperor of All Maladies: A Biography of Cancer*, by Siddhartha Mukherjee. I'm not terribly interested in the clinical, physiological aspects of cancer. I'm more interested in how people have responded over the ages to cancer, the psychology of the research.

And of course as always I have a stack of poetry books I'm reading, each a different angle of the mirror, each a beating heart—mine and its, combined. The reading is one way to move through the "downness."

Another is to sit with it, meditate with it, look at the quality of my mind/body. When I drop the labels, what's there? Nothing to panic about. It's a particular kind of energy. And also, I get together with friends. This helps a great deal. And I read. Not so much to "get lost" as to see more, from different angles. And Jerry and I have just finished our marathon watch of season 2 of Downton Abby. Finally, finally, Mary and Matthew are together! That brought tears of joy to my eyes, no joke. There is as much subtlety and good writing in this series as in a great Victorian novel. Plus good acting.

And I think of the cottage, my paddle-board stored in the garage along with the kayaks and canoe, waiting for summer. That makes me smile.

12   In the Cross-hairs

I'M ON MY BACK. The red laser-beams have me in their cross-hairs. I'm staring up at where four ceiling tiles have been replaced with light-permeable photographs of an autumn scene, a creek flowing around a rock, rocks on the bank with yellow leaves plastered against them, a yellow forest behind. All is in flux. Or, this too will pass. I try to think what's meant, who chose this yellow autumn scene instead of green spring or high summer. The autumn of life, maybe. Nah.

The foot-thick door is shut with only me inside. The machine circles and steadies itself before it starts up with its soft noise that says deadly radiation is penetrating at precise angles intended to avoid major organs as much as possible. Fifteen minutes, every day, five days a week, for five weeks. I calm my outrage by reminding myself why I have to do this.

Did I mention that I don't feel well? I don't feel well. The effects of last week's chemo are still with me—vague, sickish nausea, fatigue. I started all this with a certain bravado. I would do this well, as well as possible. But now I feel tired and sick. My bravado has morphed into a kind of malaise. At least for now. Maybe a few days more away from chemo will help.

I remember a painting called "Suffering," by my 85-year-old friend, Sally Mitchell. All blocks of bright colors! I think about people with chronic illnesses, and those who take care of them. The ones who day after day get up with the same aches, same nausea, same worries they went to bed with. Anyone can endure with an end in sight. But to slog on and on. People have so many ways of working with the mind, to keep from spiraling downward: "It's God's will," "I'm tough and I'll battle this thing and win," "I'll use my sickness to gain sympathy for others who're sick." The mind wants to have some control, even if it's the control of submission.

I meditate every day, unless I feel too nauseous. None of us can get out of anything, anyway, right? We're going to be sick, we're going to hurt (psychologically and/or physically) and we're going to die. What I want is to do those things fully, look straight into what is the case, not turn away into platitudes. I suppose the most honor (attentiveness? recognition?) I can give this life is to live it fully, all its seemingly dark and light corners.

There've been so many dark corners. My brain-damaged brother, plus the two marriages I hung onto through way too many years of anger and pain. The pain of my children. I've looked and looked at all this: I'm one example of the success of hard work in therapy. Really. And then the deeper looking, on the cushion. The energy of pain has given me a lot.

The energy of happiness? Oh, there's my father's singing. Still, at 96, he can sing all of "Abdul Abulbul Amir." If you don't know it, it's a poem, ten stanzas, set to music, written in 1877 during the Russo-Turkish war. There's his recitation of poems—all of Alfred Noyes's "The Highwayman," Lewis Carroll's "Jabberwocky," huge chunks of Longfellow's "Hiawatha," all of "John Brown's Body." I could go on. The sound of words, of words elevated to the level of recitation. How could I not learn to love them?

And: there's Kelly, walking long blocks with me, picking flowers with one hand, her other hand in mine. I can still feel the cup of her fingers on mine. Scott, building great, dramatic Lego cities. Kelly practicing the piano. Scott curled in the beanbag chair watching TV. All of us camping at Kentucky Lake. All of us near each other.

As if I can manipulate anything into the happy category, or sad. As if I can meditate through anything. As if I have any answers.

Truthfully, I meditate partly because I'm in the habit. I slog on just like anyone else, I write what I can every day because this is what I do. I tell myself the same platitudes that everyone else does—"Come on, Fleda, make an effort to make life easier for those around you," or "Buck up, you'll get better later," or "Smile and you'll feel better." My wobbly bicycle stays upright by use of whatever training wheels I can think of.

Bonus: Wally's koan for today: Since birds eat worms, and you eat birds, do you eat worms?

13 Goat Cheese on Triscuits

I CAN HARDLY SEE to type. I have a bug-eye patch over my right eye, a result of yesterday's victrectomy—the floater-fulled vitreus has been sucked from my eye and the tag-ends of loose retina have been tacked down. My eye should be clear, when healed, and free of the risk of future detachments, at least as much as possible. This had to be done now rather than after the cancer treatments because the longer the detachment waits, the more permanent it becomes.

I have to lie on my stomach four hours a day, head down, to put the gas bubble in its proper place. I accomplished this this morning by lying on my airplane-horseshoe neck-brace and listening to IPR on my IPad. I am still having—unusual for radiation—a lot of nausea. Unfortunately, the radiation must strike directly at my stomach area. I have to say, nausea is one of my least favorite sensations. I am fickle as a pregnant woman about what I want to eat. I'm kind of tired of soup. But then, I'm tired of everything. I insisted on pizza last night. For lunch I ate goat cheese on Triscuits, plus sugar snap peas. I want nothing. I must eat something. Baked potatoes, white and sweet, still taste pretty good. My radiation team—so kind, so solicitous—has put together a drug cocktail that we hope will improve things a bit, but makes me groggy. Still, I'd rather sleep than feel sick. Jerry brought me a bottle of Ensure a few minutes ago—the bottom of the culinary barrel.

Nausea is like losing your internal compass, your lodestone. I've trusted the silent continent of the stomach to grow its perfect garden of enzymes. Well, heck, I've trusted the whole body to do its job, part by part. The worse I feel, the more insular my mind becomes. The more unsure that any mechanism is doing its part without my constant attention. I see now how it is with the chronically ill. The mind curls up around itself, for comfort and protection. It begins to notice every tic, every wavering from the norm. A curiosity and a worry.

One has to make regular, deliberate forays out, to remember the world. Hello to my dear friends at the Association of Writers and Writing Programs Conference in Boston this week! I have no energy to imagine being there. Kelly and her family are off to London, to visit for a couple of weeks—then she may be back here. Jerry's daughter Pam has just been here. She had breast cancer a couple of years ago, at age 40. We took a drive up Old Mission Peninsula— she and Jerry tasted wine while I hung around, breathing deeply to hold back nausea. It was good anyhow, to get out. Jerry's other daughter Amy is coming to visit. Scott's coming. This, plus all the sweet, smart, and homemade cards make me smile. And every friend's visit matters to me. And writing. I can barely see the keys, yet here I am, enlarging the type so I can go on. I have a student's work to get back to her soon.

This bubble in my right eye will last about a month. Then my eye should be in good shape. I just go on, doing what comes next, which I guess is no different from what anyone does when we're well. Take care of what's in front of us at the time. I've spent my career taking care of one thing after the other, plowing through papers, getting manuscripts ready, doing what came next. What's different is that I've become patently, strikingly, lit-up-in-neon-aware of transience.

Mushy is not my style. When I was a kid, I always wanted to be the cowboy, not the sissy cowgirl with ruffles on the skirt. In my family, I figured I'd better be tough. I had a ray gun from a cereal box, one that shot baking powder. I saved for weeks to get it. Now I'm getting my ray gun and my cowboy outfit back out from moth-balls. That will be me you see, outside the corral, reeling with nausea, but chasing off the wolves all the same.

Bonus: Wally's koan for today: "If there were no inside, would you still want to go outside?"

14 The Astounding Cancer Hat

THIS WEEK HAS BEEN, well, not so easy. My eye has been a bit sore and fuzzy from the vitrectomy (My spell-check wanted to call it a vasectomy, but no), and I'll have this large gas bubble in front of my vision for the next few weeks. Imagine me typing this in 18-point just so I can see it. My face two inches from the keys.

Then this nausea. Just watching my children swing used to make me nauseated. Once Dennis and I went on an all-day fishing trip off the coast of Florida and I began throwing up Grape Nuts and Dramamine before we were out of the harbor. Once I rode three rides at Busch Gardens with Jerry and his daughter Pam and was sick to my stomach for two days after.

My radiation doctor gave me Friday off because I looked so peaked, and I missed all but a couple of hours of a long-awaited meditation retreat lying in bed instead. There was talk of lowering the area of radiation to miss my stomach, but that would be risky. But I'm happy to report that it appears we (I'm now a "we") have come up with a cocktail of drugs that keep me feeling pretty decent. The addition of a small amount of steroid to the mix seems to settle my stomach. I don't question why or whether this will last; I'm just grateful. This morning, to celebrate, I came down to breakfast wearing my funny hat, made by my friend Devon in Delaware.

My lord what a hat! It's peaked, like an elf's hat, with little circular flowers on it. She must have spent weeks and weeks on the intricate knitting, the bands of slightly different yellows, pinks, and greens. Then she sent it, and I had to admit to her, it was way too big. It hung over my head, over my eyes, more like a teepee. I like to think she was so in love with the project she got carried away. Then she took it back and essentially re-made it. It's a showpiece.

Speaking of hats, I have a bunch of cancer-hats, plus the wig. I wear the wig out, but at home the hats are more comfortable. When you have to look at yourself wan and bald, you think a lot about apparel, what would help.

15 Like Something Skinned

SNOW, SNOW, SNOW. THE first day of Spring. The theme for today is unpredictability. I've been weak, needing long naps, and was about to write about weakness, when I find out my white and red blood counts are climbing back up. Woe is me, how can I get a trajectory going here? Once again I watch my body do things I have apparently little control over.

Control. In the past, I've had good reason to keep chaos at bay. Kelly used to call me "the rock," which isn't altogether the best of epithets, for a mom. Steady and reliable, yes, but wouldn't one want to see the vulnerability, the uncertainty, to see how it might be managed?

Most of my life my nerves have been, as the poet Anne Carson puts it, "open to the air like something skinned." Like many writers, I've been pretty smart in figuring out how to buffer, how to let the words hold me—or hold the words, my sheaf of arrows. It's harder to buffer—for any of us—when things change so obviously quickly. I'm not complaining. I'm just looking at this. I'm looking at this through the lens of the visits of Kelly, Pam, and Scott. Jerry's daughter Amy will be along next week. A change: they're all here mid-winter (not usual). Because they love us.

I found Scott some plastic bags to put on his tennis shoes, and he and Jerry got the snow dug out and blown. Scott stayed almost a week: snow delayed his flight. But he works with Big Data stuff and can click from the wilds of northern Michigan to California and India. But I'm aware especially of just being taken care of. Looking at my big, quite handsome, gray-haired son and knowing he's brought not only several seasons of BBC Sherlock, but his own precious self. I'm seeing all of us—in my present particular awareness–as flesh, all breaking down at its various rates, all joyously hung in this void or un-void where we just go on, watching out for each other.

I remember my Nana, who, it seemed to me then, wanted every-thing perfect—house, garden, flowers in vases, dinner table, yard. She used to pinch my cheeks because she said they didn't have enough color. She was dismayed about my tomboyish clothes. Then she had a stroke. One of the last things I remember before they moved her to a retirement home in Colorado was her asking me to be sure the hair on her chin got plucked after she died, for the funeral. Keeping what control she could. How would I be, how will I be, if my life comes to that?

I have been one to plan, arrange, amass credentials. But now I'm reading *The Elegance of the Hedgehog,* by Murial Barbery. (I recom-mend it!) The main character, Renee Michel, a French concierge, intelligent and educated far beyond her station, has been flip-ping through her sister's pretentious dissertation on William of Ockham. Renee says:

> The quest for meaning and beauty is hardly a sign that man has an elevated nature, that by leaving behind his animal impulses he will go on to find the justification of his existence in the enlightenment of the spirit: no, it is a primed weapon at the service of a trivial and material goal. And *when the weapon becomes its own subject* [my ital.], this is the simple conse-quence of the specific neuronal wiring that distinguishes us from other animals; by allowing us to survive, the efficiency of intelligence also offers us the possibility of complexity without foundation, thought without usefulness, and beauty without purpose. It's like a computer bug, a consequence

without consequence of the subtlety of our cortex, a superflu-
ous perversion making an utterly wasteful use of the means at
its disposal."

Lord, that's profound. Our very intellects roiling around, wasting
themselves on needless complexity. Sometimes it's good for a belly
laugh, those rare times when when we see our pretentiousness, our
need to arrange and control.

What I learned from Christianity has often been over-simplified
to "Let go and let God." Then it appeared to me that the wildly
ambiguous word God is like a door-stop in front of the openness. I
won't say all the time, but sometimes, the word God will appear in
a poem just at the point where looking closer might reveal a detail
that gets still closer to the essential openness. What's there? Can't
see. If I can't see, what can I see? This object, this wrinkle, this
dust. What if I look really hard at that? It won't stay stable in my
mind because my mind made up what it is. That's okay. Maybe if
I'm lucky, I can catch the exact intersection, the surprise between
what my mind's doing and what I think, *think,* is out there.

Not to get all apocalyptic. But when one's "ordered" life is
disrupted, one does ponder like this. Oddly, as I feel less "substantial," it's a joyful feeling. Light. I don't HAVE to be substantial, do
I? Or in charge. I'm tired of that.

16 Tribute to Jerry

WELL OVER TWO DECADES ago, I'd just left my dangerously destructive second marriage. I was terrified of another relationship, but lonely as hell. There was Jerry, my colleague in the English Department for lo those many years, himself having just eased out of a sad marriage. In our advance-and-retreat pas-de-deux, he was the perfect, gracious gentleman, leaving me all the time I needed to see what I needed. My head screamed "NO!" My heart played interception. "I will never hurt you," he said. Verily, he spake the truth.

Jerry's the one you want with you if you are really sick, and he is the one you want with you if you want to have a good time. He's interested in most everything except science, science-fiction, pretentious literary theory, and animated feature films. He's been a sessions singer in Nashville, he's dated Pat Boone's sister, had drinks with Robert Penn Warren, watched Elvis rehearse. He's remodeled an old farmhouse, coached his daughters' softball teams, farmed his 15 acres, as well as fronted a successful rock and roll band ("Jerry and the Juveniles") while chairing a 60-member English Department, writing and editing seven books, being general editor of the works of the eighteenth century writer Tobias Smollett.. . . well, just to give him his due, before I get to what I really want to say.

Jerry is nurturing. He'll rub my feet until his hands get numb. He's downstairs right now doing the laundry. He washes and folds it all, every week. He washes the dishes. (I cook! I'm not useless). He likes to do these things. He's a detail person. When I got sick, he took my car to get the snow tires on, he took it in for service, filled it up with gas. He's run dozens and dozens of errands for me. He wants to go to every daily radiation treatment, just to be with me. But he's not cloying. He lines up my multitudinous pills for me and reminds me, but that's because he knows how I am. He steps back if he thinks I've had enough of management, or closeness.

He respects me. He's not interested in Buddhism, but he's supported my practice by cheerfully sending me off to retreats and has *never* made one disparaging or dismissive comment.

He's read and helped me edit almost every word I've written.

He knows how to take care of himself. He's going semi-weekly to a caregiver's support group. So far, he's the only one who shows up, but he likes the woman, so they keep talking. He has his own health issues which have been a trial for him for over two years— complicated neuropathy with possible spinal involvement, plus. He doesn't martyr himself on the altar of my cancer. He's doing what he can for himself with hopes that we can get to Mayo and see what the heck's going on with him as soon as I'm through with all this.

When I found that I'd need to have eye surgery just as I was starting cancer treatment, he came with me to the retinal surgeon's office. We were alone, waiting for the surgeon to come in. He looked up at me. Tears started down his cheeks. "You are so strong," he said. "And I see you sitting there looking so small and vulnerable. It hurts me."

So basically, this is in praise of our being able to cry together, which we've done face-to-face with fear, when it comes up, with sadness, when it comes up, and with sheer frustration, when it comes up. This is in praise of a man who tells me every day how beautiful I am, with my silly chemo hats and abdomen full of puncture scars, who runs his hand over my barely furry scalp as if I were Cleopatra.

I've gotten irritated with him—he's a tortoise and I'm a hare—I've gotten frustrated by his meticulous attention to lining up the details in order. But not once, in 21 years of marriage, have I regretted marrying him. We've been good for each other. We still are. Thank you, Jerry, for waiting with infinite patience until the moment—over two years from our first beer together—when I finally pled, "Oh, please PLEASE marry me!"

17   That Damnable Monosyllable

YESTERDAY MORNING WE WERE in a snow-globe of lake-effect fluff, drifting all over. It was beautiful. To me these days, most things are, well, a revelation, meaning that being alive is—shall I say just great? That sounds so Panglossian. I mean it's all okay, snow or sun, no joke. It's April 3. Melting snow is soaking some moisture down where it needs to be, after our dry, dry summer last year. The tart cherries should be good this year. And our two good friends from Traverse City, Myrna and Joan, got married in D.C. yesterday after 20 years living as a committed gay couple with no legal protections or civil recognition. A great day for them—ages 72 and 80. Kelly, who lives in D.C., was able to attend, to represent us and herself.

And I finished my 25 sessions of daily radiation yesterday. I imagine I feel better already, not having those rays daily directed straight at my digestive system. I've felt pretty punk most of the time, and increasingly tired. I'm taking long afternoon naps and going to bed early. Next is three weeks (3 sessions) of "internal" radiation, to target the scar tissue around the hysterectomy surgery. Then three rounds, three weeks apart, of chemo again.

Will I be "cured?" The radiation oncologist carefully says we "hope to keep the cancer away." This is accurate. It was always accurate even when I didn't know it, right? We moment-by-moment, collapse and resurrect, collapse and resurrect. We hope the balance hangs in our favor a good long while. The mind is good at ignoring, mostly, our end. But at some cost, it seems to me now. There is a "dearest freshness deep down things," as the poet Hopkins puts it, that's only touched when our feet are (metaphorically, at least) unshod, when they can feel the soil we come from and return to.

Jerry's daughter Amy visited this last week. She teaches at Lane College in Eugene, Oregon, and gave up most of her spring break to be here for me and for her dad. I was too tired to do much more than take a jaunt to the local museum and go out to eat once, but it was great to have her here. She built me a little Buddha stand. It's seven inches tall and holds my small statue that sits in the corner by my mat and bench. I'm not much for images or ritual, but it doesn't hurt to have the little man perched there, reminding me to stay at it.

I'm not a Christian anymore, maybe. Depending on how you mean it. I still have a deep affection for the Church. I've loved its images, its rituals, its glorious language. After my years on the cushion, those images haven't gone away. Who would want them to? At this point, to me, they seem a good story, but not the whole story. In the same way, I suspect, that the great mystics saw through all that, to the plain shining, gritty truth of things, that exists with or without my or anyone else's smart-ass input.

I just read a fine interview with Christian Wiman, the editor of *Poetry Magazine*, by my old friend Jeanne Murray Walker in *Image Magazine*. Wiman says, "Silence is the necessary soil for poetry, and the blight that eats into our surest words. Silence is the only sound God ever makes, and it is the often crushing condition of his absence. Every once in a while you encounter a work of art that silence has truly and permanently entered, like fallen autumn leaves that, riddled with holes, are on their way to being entirely light."

Corollary Issue: *Why I Have this Cancer*: Thank heaven for the researchers and curers. That's not what I mean. I mean metaphysically why. I think of Job, who refused to ask. And I think of this, from John Donne's Sermon CXXX:

It is an execrable and damnable monosyllable,
why; it exasperates God, ruins us.

18   Ways of Seeing

APRIL 10TH, SNOW AGAIN, dark and heavy skies. I feel the long, long stretch of this. In spite of my miraculous, sensitive oncologists, the angelic nurses and staff—still, it's my body and I'm tired. And weary, which is different. They said the five weeks of radiation would be easier than chemo, but no. Even with the cocktail of drugs, I feel bad. I'm still taking them.

Now I'm having the "internal" radiation once a week, targeted at internal scar tissue where cancer cells might lurk. They wheel me into an isolation chamber, insert a rod inside me, and lock me in for about five minutes. It's so toxic in there, no one can come in until they shut the machine off.

No problem, they said: this time we're hitting below your stomach. Shouldn't bother you. Maybe it hasn't. Maybe my extreme fatigue is accumulated from the total radiation. I spent last Saturday and Sunday lying on the sofa sleeping, reading a bit, and sleeping some more. The measure of my fatigue is whether or not I can *make* myself get on the treadmill for a mere 20 minutes. Some days not.

The word "bravery" has always annoyed me when it comes to major illness. After all, you get sick, you do what you have to do. You take the pills, you get the treatments. Bravery has nothing to do with it. Bravery is when you face something you're scared of, in hopes of making things better. You fight dragons, you rescue a child from an oncoming truck, you give a speech in front of thousands. You divorce your abusive husband.

I should have recognized this other kind of bravery: you drag yourself out of bed even when you feel like warmed-over frozen pizza, and you put on makeup and you coordinate your chemo hat with your outfit even when you're going to be at your desk all day. You get your work done, if slowly. If you have no poems coming, you read and make notes. You read. The main thing is, after months of this, it does seem to take bravery to *stay in the world.* Maybe that's not specifically bravery, since the will to live is pretty potent, and until our bodies tell us otherwise, we fight tooth and nail to stay in the world. Still, the Sisyphean dailiness of this fatigue seems to call for a kind of bravery.

There's the launch party at the library on Friday for the book I told you about, *Growing Old In Poetry: Two Poets, Two Lives.* I was feeling better when I set this all up, but the party lasts only two hours, and I'm looking forward to it. Since it's an e-book, we're calling the party "Books in Space." We'll have Syd, my co-author with us on YouTube, plus the editor of Autumn House Press, Michael Simms, on Skype, the library staff will be there to help people download the book, and we may even be on local TV.

So what about these e-books? How dare we undermine our precious independent bookstores, that I value so dearly? I'm thinking fear is not the way we'll move into this brave new world. Did DVDs wreck the movie business? A lot of us are buying real books and will continue to. I'm reading four actual, paper books at present: Syd's new collection of poetry: *I Was Thinking of Beauty;* Albert Goldbarth's older collection of poems, *Saving Lives;* my former student Erin Coughlin Hollowell's first collection of poems, *Pause, Traveler;* Kent Haruf's *Benediction* (all his books are made of solid earth and will save your jaded soul)—and then I'm also reading Barrie Jean Borich's *Body Geographic* on my iPad (If you love Chicago, read this book). Jerry and I pass books and the Kindle and the iPad back and forth. I prefer books. I do. But in bed, and traveling, it's easier to hold the iPad open, and it stores a lot of books.

This was about fatigue, wasn't it? It was easy to segue to books, since when there's no energy at present to shape this life, the one lying here on the couch, there's always another life, another person's telling, to see into. What's "real"? The poems are real, the fabricated tales are as real as those we think *aren't* fabricated. None "true," all "true." We see into and through lives, we stretch our perceptions. Non-fiction, fiction, poems: all ways of seeing. The accumulation is a kind of energy of its own.

19 Cards and Radishes

ACH, JUST AS LITTLE hairs are sprouting on my head and my eyebrows are almost visible, I'll be starting chemo again on Tuesday! At least now I have proof that spring comes, even though the chemo will again blast away my body's current efforts toward regeneration. Of course that's the idea.

I feel quite a bit better. It's been nearly three weeks since my last daily radiation. Friday I have my last internal radiation. I've cut down on the array of pills I take to control nausea. There are still faint wisps of it, but fewer every day. I feel less weak, though I wouldn't say strong. Yesterday I walked for 30 minutes, which seems to be my limit.

In the midst of our personal troubles, there's the horrible bombing in Boston. After 9/11, I was asked to write a piece for the newspaper, as Delaware poet laureate, about why people turn to poetry at such times—which we do. We quote poems to each other; we write poems. Poetry, even for those who wouldn't touch it with a ten-foot pole otherwise, is our communal way of speaking of mystery, of what we can't understand, of grief there are no words for. Poetry can point toward what we mean, can at least touch the hem of what we feel.

Sometimes I read back through the cards and poems I've gotten this winter. I keep them in a basket (well, they've spilled over) which was also a gift, filled with chemo-type foods, gum, lotions, etc.

When the winter chrysanthemums go,
there is nothing to write about
but radishes
—Basho (1644-1694)

Coming back—
there are so many pathways
through the spring grass
—Buson (1716-1783)

Basho and Buson knew that what is, is simply what is. Celebrate that.

And:

With a love like that
you know you should be gl—ad
yeah, yeah, yeah, yee-aaaaahhhhh
—McCartney/Lennon, The Beatles, 1963

And hand-made postcards. One reads "I know that / hope is the hardest/ love we carry." –Jane Hirshfield. How much is inside those few words. We know the truth of this, "hard" and "hope" in the same line. Nothing is harder than to hope for someone we love.

And a Brickmobile—a postcard of a car made of bricks—with a full description on the back and the note, "Wishing you 900 lbs. of endurance and a V8 spirit."

And loons (representing Jerry and me) from Joan and Myrna who send a hand-made card every week. And dozens of cards from my sister. She knows what cards can mean. She had a (benign) brain tumor ten years ago that was so large that removing it wrecked her pituitary gland. She lay in a coma for months afterward, and has had multiple health problems ever since. The cards kept her spirits up, still do. She sent me one every day for months. I'm her big sister. How can you ever outgrow the old feeling, the two of you pouring Corn Flakes in the morning before heading for the creek, two cowboys on the hunt for the bad guys. Two very small bodies curled together under the covers while all hell is breaking loose with your parents?

Millie always says I'm supposed to do things first, so she can see how it's done. Well, she idealizes, but when I think of my life, as I write it now, I guess it's a guide. It's how I'm doing it. Not to follow, but to have this version of what one person does to get through. As for Millie—Did you know that if you slam your finger in a door, your pituitary tells the adrenal glands to pump out adrenalin to raise your blood pressure, to cope with the assault? Even a little thing like that, or sitting in the park on a blanket and getting too chilled, when she doesn't have extra Prednisone right away, can cause the blood pressure to drop almost to death. This has happened to her several times. She's living this unexpected life she has with such grace, such kindness. So many cards sent.

I have never been much of a card-sender. But indeed, it means more than I thought, to get that actual, physical object with actual handwriting on it. Someone thought of me, not just fleetingly, but deeply enough to find a card, or make a card, and write a note on it, and put it in an envelope and mail it. That lovely act of attention.

20   A Formal Feeling Comes

MONDAY WAS GLORIOUS. FINALLY the nausea from radiation wore itself out, the sun shone with the bright surprise that I associate only with northern Michigan. It got up to almost 60. Jerry and I raked a bit of the winter debris from our miniscule yard, shoveled the last of the snow out from under the hydrangea and azaleas, chopped up the ice underneath, and when I got tired (quickly), I sat in a lawn chair for half an hour letting the sun blast away on my face. In the afternoon, we went downtown to see *Quartet* (I loved it: with Maggie Smith, and Dustin Hoffman's debut as director/producer). We ate downtown, a *normal* meal, and I had my first glass of wine in months.

Fluctuation: Tuesday, back to chemo. I don't have a port in my chest. The doctor and I decided with only six chemos, why bother, and there's some risk. So, the nurse got the needle in a vein, but apparently it was in the wall of the vein. Nothing could get through. She wiggled it around for a while. Ugh. She tried a second vein. Then she tried one on the right arm. It seemed to go in but the drip was too slow. She called in the "lower arm and hand vein specialist," who was finally able to find a good vein farther down my arm. Did you know that the farther toward the extremities you go, the more sensitive the body is? Hands, feet, full of nerve endings. But after it was in, all was well. I slept for most of the four hours of drip—the Benedryl knocked me out.

I think I snored. There were four others there. I felt bad about it, but they all swore I didn't.

Monday was Earth Day, and I was thinking, what *is* all this writing, this general passion for some sort of artistic spilling of the gut? I sometimes feel foolish, or useless, making my writing a higher priority than joining the groups fighting to save our environment.

No. Not "the environment." They're fighting to keep Asian carp out of the Great Lakes, they're fighting to save a 300-year-old tree from the road crews. "Heaven is precision," says Christian Wiman. "What I crave is writing that gets right down to the nub of Now."

As the late, great James Wright said, "I want the pure, clear word." This is the thing. The immediate, personal word. The lyric impulse.

The needle in a vein.

Wiman reminds us (in his book, *My Bright Abyss: the Meditations of a Believer*), that it was the pure lyric spirit of the poet Osip Mandelstam that Stalin couldn't abide, that put Mandelstam finally in a concentration camp where he died. It was, says Wiman, "the existential liberty and largess, the free-singing soul that, Stalin seemed to sense, would always slip free of the state's net. People who think poetry has no power have a very limited conception of what power means. Even now, in this corporate country, where presidents do not call up poets on the telephone, some little lyric is eating into the heart of money."

Elizabeth Bowen: "To turn from everything to one face is to find oneself face to face with everything. "

George Oppen: "I think there is no light in the world / but the world. And I think there is light."

I can't justify the books of poems—or essays—I've written, I can't justify my mornings at the computer, tapping out words that aren't trying to persuade, aren't trying to fix or mend, aren't trying to explain. They're trying to sing, I guess. They seem to want to be written, whether I win prizes with them or not.

And writing about this cancer: I use the word "about," but that's a misnomer, really. The cancer's a force behind the words. It's one of the tensions that is bound to play forevermore in my poems, even if it doesn't make an actual appearance. It does often make an appearance. It's on my mind. How to keep it in its place, so the poem doesn't lock itself down in fascination with details or wanting to narcissistically TELL ALL. In other words, how to make a true poem. Or a true essay. Or a true story. I don't have any answers. I turn to others' poems and essays—like Christian Wiman's memoir, about his cancer and his faith—where I can watch how it's done well (I think he does it well), or not so well. And turn to the masters—such as Emily Dickinson— them first and last, the words that have lasted a long time.

After great pain, a formal feeling comes –
The Nerves sit ceremonious, like Tombs –
The stiff Heart questions 'was it He, that bore,'
And 'Yesterday, or Centuries before'?

21   Empty

IF FEELS AS IF you're utterly emptied of yourself, then one day you feel yourself starting to fill up again. Or, maybe, you're a dry stalk, and you feel some green, pale at first, coming back.

This round of chemo's stayed with me for seven days. Each recovery's slower. I seem to be a bit better, now, but not quite "back." What, you ask, do I mean when I say I don't feel well? My stomach feels sour, but the main thing is tired. Not an ordinary tired—a deep, accumulative tired. Not sure how to describe it. Example: Monday I went to the hospital for my weekly blood test. I had to wait maybe 20 minutes (unusual). Normally, I grab anything with print on it and read it, even a *Sports Illustrated*. But I just sat there, hands folded in my lap as if I were 95, waiting for the next thing. After dinner I stretched out on the sofa at 7:30 and didn't get up until we made our way upstairs to bed. Gravity announces itself with a ferocity. I just want to lie down.

Tuesday I couldn't even get through my little stretching routine in the morning, and instead of meditating, once again I went back to bed. I have to choose which one or two things I'll do in one day. If I go out, I can only run one or two errands before I want to come home and lie down.

After the steroids and anti-nausea pills wear off, after the first three days, I crash, and often have a little cry the next night. For at least a week, my mouth feels sourly metallic and a bit numb, especially the tip of my tongue. I seem to want salt and citrus right now; other tastes are either flat or flatly obnoxious. After years of eating salads with dinner, I can't abide them. It's as if I were pregnant. Things I want I really want, and things I don't, I hate. Monday night I craved multigrain chips and avocado dip. I bought them, ate too many, felt sick and could hardly eat supper. So then my whole digestive system was in an uproar.

But what do you really want to know? How this is for me, how this matters to me? Didn't Proust build four volumes on the meaning of the taste and texture of a madeline, the memories that came up when confronted by such objects of the past? I am not yet philosophical. It's too soon. I can tell you that when I'm a husk of myself, I do what I do, one thing after the other, that's all. My vision shrinks to this, and then this—not in an enlightened way, but dulled, self-absorbed. Blank to all but my stomach, or what I call fatigue, for lack of a better word.

Nothing clever or allusive today. I don't have the energy.

22   Fluctuate

I PULLED OUT MY wobbly bicycle and pumped up the tires! I rode around the neighborhood! Only a few blocks, but it was a matter of convincing myself I could do it. It was good for me, to feel myself headed down the street as always, nothing changed. Well, everything changed, but that's beside the point.

This is my week of theoretical reprieve before chemo next Tuesday, but I retain more of the bad effects than from previous chemos. Some days I could ride my bike a little if I had the mind to. Mostly not. One morning I'll feel pretty good, but by afternoon, I feel tired and sick. I felt good Monday, but Monday night I had to take a nausea pill. Still, I am much better.

It helps me to do things the same as always. I look in the mirror in the mornings and I see a stranger with no hair, one who's wearing glasses for now, at least. Glasses, I should mention, that are the wrong prescription since my eye surgery (and maybe the chemo), but it's too soon to change them. After chemo's all over, they tell me. Chemo may change my prescription! My mind tells me I'm healthy as a horse, as I've always thought, and can do anything I want to. Then the fatigue sets in. I pick a few weeds from the yard and have to sit in a lawn chair to recuperate. Still, in my mind, I'm fine, except for this cancer thing, which I've never seen and never felt. No wonder it's hard to believe in. The treatments aren't hard to believe in, however.

I pick up *0, Vanity Fair, Self,* in the doctors' waiting rooms. Which lipstick, bronzer, haircut? Which boots? Which "look" is the right one? Basically what we think others think of us, right? Our image of ourselves reflected in the expressions of others. When really, it's all us. All our own minds. Why do I not go around bare-headed bald? Because (A) it's chilly; and (B) I just want to look like me, as I said. This is me. I am the same person. Well, maybe, except for THIS.

I like(d) the way I look(ed), pretty much. After an adolescence of glasses, pimples, and insecurity, I've felt okay about myself for years. How old do I feel? My mind thinks I might be about, oh, 45. Maybe all of our ages are stored in us. Maybe we feel all ages at once. The interesting thing is that NOTHING deters me from thinking of myself as younger and healthier than I am. Not that I push myself beyond what I can do. I quit when I'm tired. Some days I drag myself up these stairs to my study. Yet to my mind, this is no more than a temporary exhaustion as if I had stayed out too late partying and now am paying the price.

I work on poems with the same sense of Forever stretching in front of me as I did when I was 30. Actually, I think this is the only way we CAN work. No one writes good poems boxed in by time. Was it Levertov who said we need at least the "illusion" of a great expanse of time to work in, whether or not we really have it?

I imagine that the mind does this until it sees its end. I don't know if this is true. I've always wanted to ask a dying person, but never had the audacity to intrude. How does it feel, to know your life is almost over? Do you believe it, really? I suppose the answers would be as varied as the people I ask.

I feel unconcerned in an odd way with my own ending. Just as I feel unconcerned, oddly, with my illness. All evidence points to its reality. I know it must be true. But I have a sense of enduring this punishment of treatments like a child sent to her room, just waiting it out, knowing she's innocent. Or knowing she's being punished more than she deserves. Or, knowing the punishment has nothing to do with the crime.

What do I disavow? My definition as a sick person, one who can't ride a bicycle?

It seems deeper than that. It's doesn't feel like disavowing. There's some sense, beyond fears, of ongoingness. I'm not talking about conventional heaven or anything like that. A sense that something, which includes me, is ongoing in a very interesting way, and all I can do is stay tuned.

23 Alternatives

YESTERDAY WE WERE EATING breakfast, getting ready to leave for my next chemo, when the oncologist's office called to say they'd just gotten Monday's blood test results, and my counts were too low. I have to postpone for at least a week. I can't tell you how disappointed I/we were. I had the magical date, June 4, when I'd be finished, and now it's June 11, barring other delays.

Maybe the fact that we ate out Saturday night and I got what was probably food poisoning and spent the night with vomiting and diarrhea lowered my counts. Or maybe because my counts were low, I had less tolerance for food bacteria. Who knows? I'm trying to cheer myself up by noting that I have another week of feeling well before the next round.

This is such a long haul. If I'd chosen a clinical trial, I'd be about done now: one arm of the trial was six chemos, no radiation. The other was five weeks of daily radiation with four chemos. The trial was to find out if radiation is necessary at all. (Since that study began, evidence has been mounting that, yes indeed, radiation improves the odds.) My oncologist is on the Board of that huge national study. However, I chose his standard treatment—three chemos, five weeks' daily radiation followed by three weekly internal radiation, then three more chemos. The full blast. Metastasized cancer's nothing to gamble with.

A friend who relies a great deal on alternative medicine could not understand why I went, seemingly unquestioningly, with what I was told, rather than investigate other therapies. I look at it this way. If I'd just been told I have blockages in three out of four of my heart arteries and the fourth didn't look so good, either, I wouldn't start a diet and exercise routine to cure it. Too late for that. Move fast, hit hard. If I'd known years ago I was on the verge of cancer, I would've tried every food and exercise routine that seemed plausible. Also, if I'd been told I was hopeless, I'd go for the best alternative plan I could find.

As it is, I'm seeing a chiropractor whose treatments are statistically unproven. He says the very subtle manipulation of nerves will boost the immune system. I think I feel better, it seems I breathe more deeply. Maybe all in my head, but it can't hurt. When I started mediating all those years ago, a lot of people sneered at it. You know, the Maharishi Yogi and his hippie followers, the incense and robes. Now that we can watch brainwaves in action, doctors as well as popular magazines recommend it.

Maybe if I had a lesser cancer. But no, I think I'd follow my oncologist's advice even then. I agree that the drug companies influence treatment. They support studies that are likely biased in their direction. On the other hand, if some non-corporate lone wolf came up with an alternative treatment that *worked* over and over (not once, not twice, but statistically significantly), I'm convinced there'd be droves of scientists and doctors dying to make a name for themselves by running the studies, with control groups, and writing the articles. Even the drug companies would find a way to make money from it.

"What do you call an alternative medicine that works? Medicine." This comes from Scott.

I'm not going to rely on anecdotal evidence. Cancers are as different as people. Sometimes people heal spontaneously. That does happen. I've no doubt some foods have cured some people. And that healing rituals have cured some people. Who knows what mysterious things go on in the body? I'm deeply grateful for the many prayers offered for my recovery. I feel buoyed and supported, healed in some way, by them. I'm drinking lots of green tea, eating well, and getting as much exercise as I can. When the treatments are over, I'll keep that up.

When the treatments are over…now that I'm nearing the end—oh well, less near than I thought—the fear rises in me a bit more. As long as I'm having chemo, something's being done. That feels a bit secure. Then what? Will all the cancer be dead? Will the same conditions that caused it cause it again? No one knows. But frankly, no one knows anything much. We're the product of so many causes and conditions we can't begin to know them all.

It seems all we can do is rely on what seems most reliable.

I do what I can. I trust the help of those who seem trustworthy. This is my life, right now. The sun's shining and it's finally warming up again. Our tulips are blooming. I'm going to take a walk.

24 What I Haven't Said

SUNDAY WAS GLORIOUS. JERRY and I drove to Empire and walked on the Lake Michigan beach, kicking our warmth-deprived feet in the white sand, picking up rocks, looking over at the pale cliff of Sleeping Bear Dunes, and then we drove to the tiny resort town of Glen Arbor a few miles away and walked that beach. We ate lunch at an outside table. There is a feeling you get when you've been confined by illness. You're watching yourself. "Look, I'm having lunch out here on the deck. Look, I'm having a fish sandwich. Look at me, with my napkin and iced tea."

Nothing but transitions: Tuesday—yesterday—was my second-to-last chemo, a week late. My platelet score was still one point too low, but the decision was to go ahead, but lower the dose of carbo-platin a bit. There's no guarantee that I'll be able to have the next chemo in 3 weeks. It might be 4 again. But we can hope. It's better to have them as close together as possible. And there was another struggle with the IV. My thin, slippery, and tired veins eluded the first three efforts. The expert was called in again and after a lot of careful tracing up and down my arm, tapping and thinking, she inserted the needle once into the right place. But it was a tender vein and I needed a warm pack on it. Total drip time is about 4 ½ hours.

So, I asked my oncologist. What happens when I'm finished? What do you look for and how often do you check? He said I'll have a scan at 6 months, another at a year, and one a year after that. "But frankly," he says, "it doesn't matter. We hit you hard with this treatment because, considering your level of cancer, if it comes back, it will take your life."

Oh.

We talk about statistics while my mind is still reeling. "I told you not to pay any attention to statistics," he says. "You're not a statistic."

Okay, here's what I haven't said before: the 5-year (typical marker) survival rate for this cancer is 35-65% (I've also been told by the radiation oncologist that it's probably as high as 85% these days). But the numbers aren't clustered around 50%. There's a huge standard deviation, so these rates are made up of survivors widely scattered along the continuum, many of those people obese, with diabetes and other health problems.

Back to the oncologist: "You're thin, you have good health habits. I told you before you shouldn't have this cancer. I have good expectations (Did he use those exact words? I wish I could remember) for you to be in that upper group." I'm always scared when he walks into the room. Time to face the music. He's tall, youngish but with gray hair, an air of take-no-prisoners authority. He's good with the unvarnished truth, but then he backs up, a bit apologetically, and tries to varnish it a little. But this is the way he is—a surgeon and researcher. But I'm also grateful. There's a peculiar relaxation in knowing that this is it. There's no ambiguity. If it comes back, there may be ways to retard its growth for a while, but that's all.

I don't think it will come back. That's the truth. That's what my mind and body tell me.

But: Transition again: "Mad Men's" opening sequence has a silhouette of a man falling, with a tall corporate building in the background. He doesn't begin from anywhere; he doesn't end anywhere. He's just falling. Entirely unmoored. Nothing to hang onto. Everything changing constantly.

We love what we love. We want it—and ourselves—to last. But what is it we want to last? A collection of thoughts about who we are. Even they change. But beyond the changing, what's there? God? Something else permanent? What if it's Changing that's beyond Changing? That's not so bad, is it? Why even try to talk about this? Words play out. But it seems useful to at least let the words point toward it. Poetry is best at this. When a poem causes us to suck in our breath and have nothing to say, it's pointing. When there's no way to say what it's pointing toward, it's pointing.

Wally says he licks away a multitude of hairs every day, yet he seems to remain the same. Except for the sudden hairballs, each at a different spot on the rug.

25 I'm Shitty, Go Away

THE DOCTOR'S OFFICE JUST called. My platelet count is down to 40 (normal is 150-400). They warned me to be careful with knives, not to operate a chain saw, etc. I said I wouldn't. I may have another blood test before the weekend. My hemoglobin is way low also. I am so tired I got dressed this morning and flopped down on the bed in exhaustion from the effort. I sat down three times while changing our king-sized bed on Sunday. I sat and read all day yesterday, including an hour-long nap. Walking up stairs makes me huff and puff.

I also feel icky. "Icky," in case you're not sure, means "messy, disgusting, horrid, nasty," according to my computer thesaurus. My iPhone app, a bit more idiomatic, says "crappy, lousy, rotten, shitty, stinky, probably from 1935 *icky-boo*, 'sickly, nauseated,' probably baby-talk elaboration of sick." My friend Anne-Marie gets pretty close in guessing what it's like—like unto the feeling you have the next day if you've had way too much to drink the day before. Your body buzzes. It feels, well, of course, poisoned. Every cell is in rebellion. The skin's sensitive. There's a slight sense of nausea and food is wretched to contemplate. The air around you is unsettled, kind of a "whump, whump" feeling, as if you were in a car with one window a little open in the back.

The inside of my mouth feels a bit numb as well as bad-tasting. The taste buds aren't working right. Oh well, I've said this before. Nothing new.

That's the thing. "How *are* you?" people ask. They're hoping to hear, "Oh, better now" or "Not bad, doing okay"—something to which they can then respond, "So glad to hear it." I sometimes imagine a tendency for people to want to pull away if I say "Not good at all. I still feel awful." People like me, who've always wanted to fix things, feel frustrated when we can't. But we can't. What we can do is just be present. Just be concerned, say we're sorry.

My friend Mary, who's had lymphoma, says, "When people ask you how you are, say 'I'm shitty. Go away.'" I'll bet she only *felt* like saying that.

This illness has put me in touch with someone who's had her endometrial cancer return, others who have other life-threatening illnesses. And a couple of people who are clearly dying and know it. They're me. And they're not me. We can't escape each other. I'm deeply sad, thinking of the pain and fear I see. And those (at least 50%) who're well now, who've had no return of the cancer, those I'm also separate and not separate from—where are they? I figure they're quiet about it. Maybe they don't want to alert the gods! After all, nothing's sure. At any moment.... This is the way it is, whether we see it or not.

I'm also thinking about those with chronic illnesses, those who constantly feel bad, like my sister Millie. I've been at this for nearly six months and already I feel like a bore saying how I am. Let's talk about writing, politics, anything else, okay? But really, how I feel is registering with me every minute. So when I talk about something else, this is lurking, waiting to take center stage again. Think of those who hurt or feel sick all the time! No wonder there's a withdrawal. First of all, there's no energy to shop or go to concerts or read complicated essays, and second, the attention must keep rounding back to "me, me," my illness, how I feel.

I'll feel better in a week or so. My experience has shown me this is the case. My blood counts will start to improve (I might end up having to have a transfusion to make that happen!). I may have to postpone the next (last) chemo. But it will happen, and I will start to get better.

Still, I'm giving up my always-anticipated-with-joy teaching in the residency of the Rainier Writing Program this summer. I don't think I have the energy to stay with it all day long, day after day. It's ten days of non-stop workshops and classes, intense conversations, readings, parties. Just can't do it. I can't even imagine walking the half-mile, over and over, up the hill from the faculty apartments to the classroom building. I'll miss the faculty—we've been together for eight years now and dearly love each other—and the students. A lot. I'll miss the mental stimulation. But I think of this as temporary. I'll be back next year.

And I keep writing stuff, which has saved my soul over and over again. It shapes this "me" as much as any damn fool collection of errant cells.

26 Someone Else's Territory

ANOTHER EFFORT TO FIND a cooperative vein yesterday. Two tries this time. Did you know that warming the arm makes the veins easier to find and penetrate? The trivia I'm learning.

This was for a transfusion of one unit of red blood cells. I got to the hospital at 10:45, as requested, but the actual transfusion didn't begin until after 1:30! They had to send a vial of blood to be typed and cross-checked for antibodies, and apparently the lab was slow that day. It was 3:50 and I'd read half of *The Marriage Plot* before Jerry picked me up.

I'm supposed to feel perkier by this afternoon. I'm exhausted this morning. I think yesterday made me tireder than I thought. The waiting, the searching for a good vein—and on top of it all, my dear brother-in-law John (Millie's husband!), was having one of the most complicated and serious surgeries there is, at the University of Michigan Hospital in Ann Arbor. It's called the Whipple procedure, and is to head off incipient (or early stage) pancreatic cancer. They removed one-third of his pancreas, part of his stomach, gall bladder, duodenum, and bile duct. He's doing well, by the way, and the tests so far haven't shown active malignancy. Hooray for that.

Not to pass by this fact so blithely. There've been all these more dramatic issues, Millie's tumor, my cancer, and there's John, the always-kind, always on top of things, caregiver who gets sick, really sick, maybe. This is what happens sometimes. The one who helps gets sick. From the strain? I can't imagine how it's been for him the last ten years. He's literally saved Millie's life over and over by being alert, researching the best doctors, reading all the articles the doctors ought to have read and sometimes haven't, and tactfully suggesting what might be done next. So, praise be that he seems to be okay after all. False alarm, maybe, that ended up taking half his innards with it.

Two things occur to me. One is how, since we don't die young so much these days from the old diseases, we can grow old, and suddenly all around us is illness and the sorrow of illness, barely staved off by modern medicine. This is *so* true in my family the last few years that it feels almost traitorous to turn away into my own work. That really isn't the issue, though. It's how to be with illness. Based on my own, I'd say—and have said, forgive me for repeating—the best thing we can do for each other is to be emotionally present. Not leaning toward identification, which is smothering, and not leaning away, which is escaping. Just being there. It may be possible to avoid burnout that way. Although if we care, there's bound to be a point where we just want to get the heck out of there and live our own lives. What can we do but recognize that? We're human.

The other thing is the writing. I've written a few poems that concern themselves with Millie's surgery and subsequent difficulties. There's a necessary objectification in this that feels like betrayal. How can one dip into someone else's deeply personal and indescribable suffering and bring it to words?

It's not any different, is it, from writing deep into anything we don't know? What DO we really know? But in this case, we're carrying our imagination down into someone else's territory. Which as writers, we can't help doing. HOW we do this, I'd say, is what matters. We don't want to usurp the pain for ourselves. There's a respect we need for this: possibly the subjunctive, possibly a third-person removal, possibly a disavowal in the work, of our ability to really know. It may require the same emotional "not leaning" I mentioned earlier.

What would that leaning look like? It would look like "me," over-laying myself on "you." My students have given me some of the most amazing "interpretations" of poems that have nothing to do with the poem. It's all about what's going on in their heads. Reverse that as a writer and that's what I'm calling identification. Not seeing what's actually there. Happens a lot in some successful writing, but maybe not in humane and accurate treatment of those we care about.

Leaning back too far, escaping, is easy to spot. You can feel the cleverness of the metaphor taking over, the way the writing is all about the writing. For whatever reason, it doesn't want to see the pain, really. It wants to play with it.

I'm leaving in a few minutes to record the next pieces for Inter-lochen Public Radio's show, "Michigan Writers on the Air." I'll be talking about Sharon Olds's *Stag's Leap*, which won the Pulit-zer this year. It's her best book, in my opinion. Olds, who's 70, by the way, writes into the pain of divorce after 32 years of what she thought was a happy marriage. Her metaphors seem to arise natu-rally. There's little self-conscious playing with her own grief, and there's no sense of trying to escape it, either. That's what I mean.

27   The Chinese Farmer's Horse

NO FINAL CHEMO THIS week. We're so disappointed. I had wanted to get this over with and start repairing, but my white blood count, especially the neutrophils, are too low. The platelet count has come up and the hemoglobin is okay, but.... The nurse said she was surprised about the white count, since I had an injection of Neulasta to prod my bone marrow into production. "It's the cumulative effect of all that radiation as well as the chemo," she said.

So, I'll tell you our rhododendrons are gorgeous this year, all soft pinks and blues. This will cheer me up. The delay made me irritable and, frankly, depressed. I didn't expect that reaction, since generally there's been a measure of equanimity with all this. Then I remembered a Zen story:

The wise Chinese farmer's horse ran off. His neighbor came to console him, but the farmer said, "Who knows what's good or bad?"

When his horse returned the next day with a herd of horses following her, the foolish neighbor came to congratulate him on his good fortune.

"Who knows what's good or bad?" said the farmer.

Then, when the farmer's son broke his leg trying to ride one of the new horses, the foolish neighbor came to console him again.

"Who knows what's good or bad," said the farmer.

*When the army passed through, conscripting men for war, they passed over
the farmer's son because of his broken leg. When the foolish man came to
congratulate the farmer that his son would be spared, again the farmer said,
"Who knows what's good or bad?"*

When does this story end? There's no fixed "good" or "bad."
They're beliefs, judgments, ideas based on limited knowledge as
well as on the inclinations of our minds.

I've been reading a lot. I haven't had energy for much else. The
above story comes from *Buddhism Plain and Simple*, by Steve
Hagen, one of the clearest and best books on the subject I've read.
Besides things I've mentioned earlier, I've read *Lady Almina and
the Real Downton Abbey* (a gift) by the Countess of Carnavon, the
current owner of the estate. I appreciated the intimate view of
the beginning of WWI and the discovery of King Tut's tomb. I've
skimmed back through *The Emperor of All Maladies,* for cancer
details for some poems. I've read *Beautiful Ruins*, by Jess Walter.
I'd read his novel, *The Zero,* several years ago. Now I'm going to
get *The Financial Lives of the Poets.* I've read Siri Hustvedt's *What I
Loved*, an amazing psychological exploration of an artist, a critic,
and their relationships. I read Gillian Flynn's *Gone Girl* and found
it richer than I'd thought it would be, in the exploration of the
way her characters construct a "self" to present to the world. And,
sigh, I have to admit I'd never read *Little Women*! So I did. It's even
more sappy and moralistic than I expected, but I dutifully slogged
my way through.

I've read a lot of poetry, of course. Right now I'm reading *Tourist in
Hell* by Eleanor Wilner. I've always admired her intelligent poems.
The poems in this book are relentlessly political but all fresh. I do,
after a while, long for more of the intimate "I." Here's the beginning of one, though, that does conjure up the personal, the disappointment that registers personally. It's called "Cold Dawn of the
Day When Bush Was Elected For a Second Term."

> *I am jealous today   of my dog   of his ignorance of all*
> *this / of his unerring instinct   for what matters and his general aesthetic*
> */ for meat   and his inability to vote / against his own best interests. . . .*

I guess the themes for today are disappointment and reading. All my life I've had my nose in a book while I've waited for disappointment to settle down in me and gradually dissipate. Then I think of Scott's own little nose in his books—*Old Yeller*, Shel Silverstein's books, *The Three Investigator* series, *Bob Fulton's Amazing Soda Pop Stretcher*, the Matthew Looney books—all for the same reasons. Not to escape—it's too easy to say that—but to burrow down into others' lives—of course they're no less real when made up—where there is necessarily some perspective. And maybe inspiration. People have read the lives of saints and martyrs for centuries for that purpose.

Good grief, this is such a small disappointment, a week's delay! But Wally the Buddha Cat says that even the smallest irritations can feel huge when looked at straight on. He says they're made of gossamer, but they sometimes look like a mouse.

28 Sharp Turn of Seasons

HOORAY! MY WHITE COUNT was 1.1. I needed 1.0, so I just squeaked by. I had my last chemo yesterday. It took two tries this time to find a decent vein. The first time the needle went in, but some scar tissue probably blocked the chemo's flow enough to cause pressure and discomfort, so the nurse went to the other arm, the most battered one, and managed to find a good spot. Although today there are little sore nodules all along the vein.

I'll continue to have blood tests for three weeks, and today I go in for a Neulasta shot to boost my white blood cell production. I'm in the "chemo phase" now, which means I'm hopped up on steroids, ready to run five miles and lift weights, and will be this crazy for three days. Usually, the great fatigue and malaise begins a day or so after that. But saying "usually" makes no sense, since each time has been different. This being the end of treatment, there was some hugging when I left. And my oncologist spent some time with me, talking about the future. You may remember his dire prediction if the cancer came back. He didn't mention that again. What he said to me, paraphrased by me:

1. Walk out of here and forget about me, forget about this place entirely. Do not spend your life worrying. You'll no doubt start to get anxious before each checkup, but until then, eat ice cream, get on your paddle board, forget all this.

2. Okay, you say you'll have a cloud over your head, but each year that goes by, the cloud will be higher up and lighter. One day you'll hardly even see it. (Lovely of him to say this.)

3. You can exercise as much as you want. Go ahead and get tired if you want. Just rest when you need to. If you can only walk a mile and you want to walk two, do it in increments. (Okay, Jerry, you can get off my back now about "doing too much.")

4. It seems that women who have a spiritual practice, a religion, do better with all this. If you do have something, you may find a much-renewed interest in that. (Little does he know…. Did I tell you, I've studied Christian theology, been a church elder— the first woman and youngest—an active Episcopalian, and now this meditation practice. "Renewed" indeed.)

Speaking of every day, today is beautiful as only northern Michigan can be. Summer is short, so every perfectly warm and sunny day strikes like a gong in the mind. It's hard not to be aware, when we know how a day like this will pass, shortly, and for that matter, how short life is. But we'd shoot ourselves—or in Jerry's and my case, pack our bags for South Carolina—if we loved only summer. It's the sharp turn of seasons, the swimming and kayaking, gradually or not so gradually, giving way to high-piled snow, a glittery rolling landscape, sharp edges blunted, bright even on dull days.

I love to walk around our neighborhood, especially in summer, when the flowers are out. I love the cracked sidewalks and each different house, all old, some beautifully restored, some ramshackle. I cannot leave them alone. I remodel each one, I offer (mental) suggestions to the owner about how to improve the façade, what paint colors would work better. This isn't very equanimous of me, my desire to edit things, but I don't care. I just watch my mind do that and watch its delight in doing it. I spend so much time with the details of poems (and prose), editing with as much precision as I can, so naturally, I edit everything. What line-break, what verb, what paint color, what flowers, will improve the aesthetics of this situation?

Oh yes, also, the galleys for my new poetry collection, *No Need of Sympathy*, from BOA Editions, are ready.

29   Wrath of God

I WANT A LARGE gothic font. I want it as emblem. This last chemo struck me like the **Wrath of God**. It took five days for my body to register the ghastly conclusive blast, but register it did—stomach and entire digestive system screaming "enough, enough." Fatigue flattened me on the couch, my entire body aching. Each day since then I've climbed one foothold up the cliff toward repair, but I can see it's going to take a long time this time.

This wickedness was much improved by the arrival in my mailbox on Monday and Tuesday of an avalanche of cards from my Delaware writer-friends. Apparently a bunch of them got together and plotted this. There were cards, books, handmade books, long letters—all manner of love. I was truly back in Delaware. I'm thinking we never "move." We carry within us our Delaware, our Michigan, our past and present. It's always present.

Before the **WOG** struck, we had one lovely day at the lake. Things are ready for the arrival of sisters, children, grandchildren. Hammock's up, screens up, dock has a coat of sealer, cottages cleaned, although not as well as in past years.

I read a lot while Jerry did stuff, which I have to say he loves to do. The book I'm reading here is *The Swerve: How the World Became Modern*, by Stephen Greenblatt. It won the Pulitzer and the National Book Award in 2011. I've underlined all over, which tells you how much it interested me. It relates to cancer and other wickedness, as I'll explain.

It's the story of Epicurus's (341-270 BC) vision of the world, how it was made available through the brilliant poem, *On the Nature of Things,* by his devotee Lucretius (1 BC), how the dominance of the Christians in Rome under Constantine (and later) destroyed the vast libraries and knowledge gained by the state's generous support of research and scholarship, so that for at least 1450 years, Lucretius was pretty much lost, until an Italian classicist-humanist named Poggio Bracciolini found a copy in a monastery in Germany, and made more copies. Gradually, what had been lost began to filter into the discourse of the time, fueling the Renaissance.

You can't just blame the Christians. A way of life was dying. So much money was being spent on foreign wars that people were poorer, less apt to care about philosophy or aesthetics. Sound familiar? Later, ignorance was so pervasive, the best minds were burned at the stake.

I tried to condense the book into one paragraph. What matters, though, is WHAT was lost. Basically, it was the valuing of reason. Okay, there was a lot for Christians to dislike in what he said: no soul, no afterlife, humans are not unique, the religious are inevitably cruel, life is a primitive battle for survival.

What was enticing in it? He described things as being composed of atoms. Things evolve to follow function. Everything comes into being as a result of a swerve. All particles would follow a straight course if at unpredictable times and places they didn't deflect slightly, no more than a shift of movement. But the main point: the highest goal of human life is the enhancement of pleasure and the reduction of pain. There were the Christians, flogging themselves and wearing hairshirts to get into heaven, and here was THIS. Listen to this one paragraph:

The greatest obstacle to pleasure is not pain; it is delusion. The principle enemies of human happiness are inordinate desire—the fantasy of attaining something that exceeds what the finite mortal world allows—and gnawing fear. Even the dreaded plague, in Lucretius' account—and his work ends with a graphic account. . . .is most horrible not only for the

suffering and death that it brings but also and still more for the "pertur-
bation and panic" that it triggers.

Lucretius thought people are unhappy because they make the
mistake of confusing the natural joy of ordinary life with a fren-
zied craving to possess, to penetrate and consume, what is in reality a dream.

So even the horrors of the Black Plague—and my own particular brand of swerve and its concomitant chemo-horrors—are not
horrible so much for themselves as for what flights of the imagination do with them. If we live within the ordinariness of the life
we have, Lucretius says, if we look squarely and calmly at the true
nature of things, deep wonder is awakened. Life, even in pain and
trouble, can be full of happiness.

I'm wondering how much access Epicurus had to Buddhist texts,
or if things arrive in the human mind collectively, without contact
with others....

Then when I couldn't concentrate enough for this heavy reading, I
read Tom Franklin's *Crooked Letter, Crooked Letter*, a heckova good
mystery that combines vivid characterization with a beautifully
constructed plot. Franklin, by the way, is married to the poet Beth
Ann Fennelly.

I'm feeling encouraged today. There are those flashes of health/
optimism that seem to arrive simultaneously in the consciousness.
Small flashes get me by for now.

30   A Good Story

I'm THINKING OF ALL the ways one might read the arc of what I've written here: (1) an opportunistic and narcissistic spilling of the guts; (2) a brave and aware facing of a serious illness; (3) evidence of the grace of God and the power of many prayers; (4) my own little self-help-by-writing-program; (5) evidence of the value of meditation; (6) my simply doing what I do, which is writing stuff down. Which of these is "true"? What have I left out?

Remember what gave me the title, "My Wobbly Bicycle"? I said we pretend there's some solidity, some predictability. But being alive is more like riding a bicycle, balancing on two thin tires. It's easy to pretend there's solidity by choosing one of the numbers above, 1-6, and ruling the others out. My way or the highway. Of course we *know* that quantum mechanics says this isn't true, but we dearly love a story arc, and the only way we get one is to ignore the others. Honestly, I don't think we can live without our stories. It's just that we take them as the Truth....

Case in point. I praised Greenblatt's *The Swerve,* that traces the beginning of modern thought primarily to the re-discovery of Lucretius' *On the Nature of Things.*" I'd read no reviews or commentary before I wrote about the book. Woe unto my students if they'd done that. An opinion/belief/point of view is only as trustworthy as the work that's gone into seeing what ELSE is out there. I need to know what the larger community of historians say about it.

There's a long review of *The Swerve* by Jim Hinch in the *L.A. Times,* another in *The Guardian,* and others that came out when the book was winning so many prizes. From Hinch: "*The Swerve* did not deserve the awards it received because it is filled with factual inaccuracies and founded upon a view of history not shared by serious scholars of the periods Greenblatt studies."

He says: "Greenblatt's vision is not true, not even remotely. As even a general reader can gather from a text as basic as Cambridge University historian George Holmes' *Oxford Illustrated History of Medieval Europe* (1988): 'Western civilization was created in medieval Europe. The forms of thought and action which we take for granted in modern Europe and America, which we have exported to other substantial portions of the globe, and from which indeed we cannot escape, were implanted in the mentalities of our ancestors in the struggles of the medieval centuries.'"

He points out that there was much less self-flagellation and hair-shirt wearing in Medieval monasteries than Greenblatt says, and much more secularism, ribaldry, drinking, etc. He gives many examples.

And the hoards of invaders that supposedly destroyed the culture of Rome? They quickly assimilated and, within decades, the areas they invaded became major centers of learning. Again, many examples.

And, he points out, "many of the supposed religious values scorned by Lucretius — faith, self-sacrifice, an identity shaped not by individual desire but by family and community — remain widespread in western and non-western cultures and are in no way inimical to human freedom and progress." Hinch says it is all a "vastly more complicated, interesting and indeterminate story. . . . Notions such as the Middle Ages and the Renaissance are little better than shorthand for arbitrarily bracketed periods of time in which certain changes in the pattern of human life are interpreted as significant and others are not."

Oh well, Greenblatt's book tells a good story, with no doubt some truth in it. I learned a lot, in any case. You can probably think of hundreds of other examples, including of course politics and religion, that lay their own private grid over the ever-flowing river of reality. I just thought of another: the new DSM-5, that re-interprets certain human behavior as mental illness, certain others not. Each edition redraws the lines.

Back to my cancer, which I've barely mentioned so far. Hooray! I'm turning my attention away from this difficult time. Has it been "difficult"? Another interpretation. It was what it was, some days I felt bad, some pretty good. If I am fortunate enough to live many years after this, how will I talk about this year? What would be a good story of it?

How am I now? Tired, tired, tired, but feeling better every day. Walking some every day, even if it's only 15 minutes. My long afternoon naps are getting a bit shorter, it seems. And I got my hearing tested yesterday—happily, the chemo didn't further damage my already bad ears. (Chemo destroys cilia in the cochlea.)

I may be finished with treatment, but I'm still hairless. Is that the truth? No, I still have a suggestion of eyebrows and little stubbles of eyelashes, the left more so than the right. You should try putting mascara on stubble. It gets all over my eyelids. Looking good has been really complicated this year.

31 PTSD

DOES ANYONE TALK ABOUT POST-can-cer-treatment? You step onto the moving walkway, put your head down, pass all the Stations of the Cross (to mix metaphors), and suddenly the voice-over says to watch your step, the walkway is ending. Feet flat on the dispassionate floor.

You've been stoic; you've looked for humor in all this. When it began, you girded your loins and took each day, horrible or not, as it came. Then it seemed you were to UN-gird your loins and be as normal as possible. Tired, yes, you knew that would be the case. Very tired for a long time.

But I did not expect to feel something akin to post-traumatic stress. I feel like wrapping myself in a blanket. It feels as if it's my body more than my mind that's reacting—but who can know the dancer from the dance? For half a year, my body's been almost poisoned to death. It's been hit day after day with deadly radiation. Of course I registered all this at the time, but part of me was numbed, maybe had to be numbed. Now my body's waking up, it seems. Holy S—!

It's been a cool spring, we haven't been at the cottage much. I haven't *yet* been swimming. I've always made a game of getting in the water as early as possible. I love swimming. But at the moment, the idea of putting on a suit and sliding almost naked into cool water gives me the shivers. I want to sit on the end of the dock in the sun and read a book. (I'll try to take the plunge this weekend. Water's 72 and I'm beginning to feel like a wimp.)

Furthermore, I'm grouchy. Something is grouchy. Irritable. I've had enough of stoicism. I have not a sprout of hair, yet, and won't have enough to blow-dry for months. My long naps mean my days are incredibly short. I'm too tired, anyhow, to meander around downtown or head out to my favorite hiking trails. Riding my bike is an idea I entertain but I haven't yet pulled it (the bike, not the idea) out of the shed.

I'm tired of being looked after, being cared for—I'm basically fiercely independent. Of course, don't misunderstand me, I still need love and caring for, and I've deeply, deeply appreciated it all the while. Still, I long to go off to a mountain cave and hibernate.

I start thinking, okay, I can move on. Then a couple of days ago I was reading, Jerry was watching a ball game, and I decided I wanted to pop some popcorn. We hadn't done that in ages. So I made a big batch and ate tons of it. In the middle of the night I woke up nauseous, started vomiting and having all the other concomitant gastric miseries. Half the night. Apparently my digestive tract is still too damaged for popcorn.

It's easy to see what's going on. I want to be normal and am now measuring myself against that standard. It irks me when I see where I am.

Well, I can read, can't I? I've finished Ali Smith's *Artful,* a series of four lectures on artfulness in fiction and poetry that she gave last year at St. Anne's College, Oxford. They're brilliantly conceived and incredibly imaginative—a ghost story as a way to experience reading and writing with awareness.

I read Elizabeth Strout's *Olive Kitteritge*, liked it more the farther I got into it. It's, in a way, a series of short stories but then again, not. Olive's life and marriage thread them together. And you develop a sense of the small town in Maine. Reminds me of Kent Meyers' wonderful *Twisted Tree*, organized a bit like that. I'm reading now Philip Levine's *The Bread of Time: Toward an Autobiography* (a gift). I'd read one or two of these essays before, but am enjoying them all a great deal, especially rereading the one about his Iowa workshop with Robert Lowell and John Berryman.

As for what I'm writing, I'm wondering again how much this cancer thing will alight in the poems. I have a few in which it's blatant, but mostly, lately, I find myself wanting to turn elsewhere. I am bored with illness, frankly. My hunch is that this experience, if I'm fortunate enough to survive it, will always remain like a boulder in the river of my writing life, taken into account in everything that gets written, even when it's not recognizable as such.

32 Recollected in Tranquility

THIS MONTH IS MY "baby" sister (14 years younger) Michelle's time at the lake. She said that since she wasn't able to visit when I was having chemo and radiation, she wanted to give me a lake-spa weekend. She's new to yoga this year, passionate about it, learning moves and practicing the techniques of "healing yoga" for herself. I had a session every day on the upstairs screened-in porch, waves lapping below, incense burning, woo-woo music on Pandora, and a little sister who loves me. If anything can cure a body, that ought to. Touch makes a huge difference, I think, not just when we're sick. A masseuse is good, but someone who loves you is even better.

AND, I finally got in the lake! I swam my usual swim to the boathouse three cottages down and back. We've always claimed the waters of our lake are the North American Lourdes, so I guess I'm doubly "cured." But I have to say, my poor muscles are weak. It was a simple swim, breast stroke, not far, but it registered all over my body. Still does.

I put on my swim cap ordered from one of the cancer sites. It's white and ruffled and comes down over even my ears. It's dopy. I look like Esther Williams. Michelle said something like, "Oh for Pete's sake, take it off." So I did. But I put it back on when there were boaters or neighbors. And the photo Michelle took of the two of us, up close, my head shining in the sun? I can't quite show anyone that one. I'm shy, obviously, about my head.

I know, I know, a lot of young (particularly) people parade their bald heads around, an act of defiance of the disease, a statement that they feel okay no matter what they look like. I don't want to be stared at, or have eyes drop when they see my head. I'm private. I'm okay with that.

I have days when I can walk over a mile, other days, like today, when I feel that chemo-y sick feeling and every movement is an effort. There seems to be no clear cause of either. My body just oscillates between okay and not-okay.

I feel somehow deficient that I haven't been turning out poems about the cancer. Other people have written really good poems about it. Though I'm reminded of what I said in my essay, "Mildred," in *Growing Old in Poetry*: you have to see things askew, you have to wait until they insinuate themselves in when the eyes are turned elsewhere. Here's Emily again:

Tell all the truth but tell it slant —
Success in Circuit lies

I'd tried to write a poem about a funny adventure with Mildred the raccoon, but it was a failure. I've tried to write poems "about" this cancer experience. I only like one or two of them, if that.

"Emotion recollected in tranquility," says Wordsworth. I say if it's tranquil, it's lost its punch and you might as well not write it at all. However, if you let it sit, it will attach itself to the shirttail of some new urgency and both will be charged by it. Why did Wordsworth say "recollected"? Anything written about is recollected. "Tranquility" because almost certainly there's much more to the poem/essay/story than the present scene yet knows. There's a breadth and depth to be brought to bear upon it. There's an assimilation that, if it happens, opens the door of the experience to let in the whole of our lives.

This relates to privacy, too, I think. If we scatter ourselves all over Facebook, if we don't allow enough pulling-back time, if we release every experience immediately into the general churning vat of conversation, how can we absorb, assimilate, and "see" what's there? I'm not talking about making meaning of it, which is more akin to preaching than to writing. I'm talking about seeing by staying with it, by continuing to watch what emerges instead of quickly ossifying it into language, photos, and emoticons.

33   Michelle's Yellow Sailboat

CANCER, CANCER, CANCER, BUT what about the rest of the world? Good grief. Things are blowing up everywhere, refugees are trying to find a safe place, England and Wales have legitimized same-sex marriage, Israel and Palestine are trying peace. Again. Reporters all over the world are clicking out the major news, hoping to write it best, get it read by the most people.

But writing is writing. No matter what we say, poem or prose, we writers always sense a lurking audience. We know what we've been praised for in the past, and we're likely to lean in that direction. But then we have this internal rudder we hope is still stronger than that. It's like sailing.

My sister Michelle has this little yellow sailboat our father built for her when she was 12 because she was afraid of his big boats, the way they lurched and leaned. He figured she would respond better to one she could manage herself. It has a cute lateen sail—you just hold the line in your hand and let the sail out and pull it in that way. The boat's been newly refurbished this year.

What does sailing has to do with anything? Something allegorical. There's the wind, which we can't control. We have to attend to it in exquisite detail. We don't want to miss a gust coming or fail to anticipate a shift. We head into the wind as closely as we can without luffing the sail. We have this object, this boat we want to move forward, but the moving forward is only a game. If we thought we needed to GET somewhere, we'd buy a monster motor. What we really want is to use our wits and attentiveness to move through the water as efficiently as possible. It's the art we're concerned with.

We're not doing the moving. But we're not passive either. We're using what comes up the best we can. We're both working and having a good time. When a big wind catches our sail and the center board's humming, we're flying almost out of control, but not quite. Not unlike my writing poems or essays. I can hope for that kind of wind, that kind of attentiveness.

This week I saw the radiation oncologist for the LAST time, it is fervently hoped. All's well. He confirmed what my regular oncologist said—it would be very bad news indeed if the cancer returned. The visit and his words left my heart, for lack of a better metaphor, in a sinking dark place, but that's no more permanent than anything is. Frankly, the feeling in my gut is no different from the times that I've had other disappointments, big blows to my ego. No different in a way than when the editor at Wesleyan called me to say the board had, finally, after much deliberation, decided not to take my manuscript. No different from even the small rejection letters. My work isn't wanted. There's a deep sense of terror, if I let myself acknowledge it. If I examine it closely, I see that it's my very self that feels at stake. Then gradually that feeling lightens and dissipates and I feel cheerful again.

What is this "self" that needs protection? Where did it come from? Where will it go? I can no more "protect" it than I can direct the wind to blow the way I want.

There's Michelle's yellow sailboat. And there's our sisters' joint birthday party. We tend to celebrate at the lake on a day close to my birthday in July. Millie's using a walker now. So each year there's joy and poignancy, this year more so since my cancer.

Someone interviewed me for a story on me and my cancer for the local newspaper. She asked me what good has come out of all this. I thought of how we tend to want to balance the scales—well, this bad thing happened but I gained this good thing. I didn't know how to answer. Things are, finally, just what they are. Is the cancer "bad"? Remember the story of the Chinese farmer? How do we know what's "good" or "bad." Our sight is short, our awareness limited. The wind (Ruach/Spirit/Holy Spirit) bloweth where it listeth.

34 Querencia

I AM SO GRATEFUL for Brown's Health Farm, a.k.a. our cottage. Nothing comes easy there, never has. You had to work at everything. It has running water now—a kitchen and bathroom—but otherwise is pretty much the same. Wood walls, no insulation, a nice little fireplace. Twenty-eight years ago, we raised the roof upstairs so that you can stand up in the two bedrooms up there. I slept on the little army cot up there when I was young. I see myself looking out the window at night, the moon through trees, and an owl. I'm sure it was an owl.

In the living room of the health farm are two couches made from cots that Uncle Richmond built 70 years ago. My sister Michelle, plus Jerry and I, bit by bit, added arms and backs. I bought the plaid fabric and Scott's wife Jen made the slipcovers with my father's old sewing machine. I figured out how to re-cover the lampshade on both lamps—one a complicated fringed Victorian thing we call the "bordello lamp." Did you know the fabric has to be cut at a 45-degree angle from the bias or it won't stretch properly over the frame? I learned the hard way. Jerry repainted all the floors. And the toy boxes, to match.

The only room downstairs with a door is what we call Aunt Cleone's room, because in her last years she slept here. We used to find her in the mornings, sitting on the edge of her bed, piles of trash around her she was sorting for recycling, although she forgot after she made the piles.

Jerry and I made the shelves which hold cute little canvas boxes for clothes. The bed's a futon we brought from Delaware, on a platform made by Rob, the son of the local Bachmann's Store ("If we don't have it, you don't need it") owner. The living room used to have a pump organ (Aunt Cleone's) but the room was so crowded we gave it to Rob. It had a broken bellow anyway. The library table is now moved into what used to be the kitchen, before the new one was built. In that middle room is the ice box that used to be turned on its side, door-less, and used as shelves, with a curtain in front of them. Jerry refinished it, turned it right-side up, had new doors made, ordered authentic hardware.

It's just the old cottage, no way to make it more than that, with its stone foundation, its tilting floors. We might have torn it down.

But. Here is the wooden medicine cabinet on the wall, with a picture of Priscilla and John Alden behind glass on its front. Why are they there? Who knows? Inside is full of perfectly preserved medicines—Campho Phenique, Brylcreem, Vapo-rub, Calomine lotion, and more—from our grandparents' time. We don't bother it. We open the door now and then and let the mixture of odors come out at us. What if these were all the medicines I had available?

Who were these ancestors, these people some of us remember, some not? We look at the hundreds of photos. We make them up in our heads. Sometimes I think, what would they think of what we think of them? They were just like us: anxious, loving, irritated, worried, tickled, afraid of dying. Having a good time, watching their kids have a good time. Their kids, who carried an image of this place with them all their lives. Whose children picked it up, changed it, and kept carrying it.

Not forever, of course. The cottage and the lake never were fixed in time, anyway. That was our idea of it. Whose idea? Mine? Grandmother's? Kelly's? Scott's? No matter.

This last week's been mostly cold and rainy, not great for the usual swimming, kayaking, biking, walking—and Kelly and family are here, all six of them. The boys went out fishing early yesterday— the best day, supposedly some sun coming—but the sky opened up and they sat for a while under the Ellsworth Bridge and then the Central Lake bridge before heading home, soaked. They did catch some pike and gar, pretty big, and threw them back. My grandson Noah would rather fish than breathe. If there are fish to be caught, he catches them. The biggest sunfish I've ever seen, for one.

We have a tradition of swimming across the lake and back every summer. Our lake is seven miles long but our cottage is at the narrowest point, a quarter mile across. In the old days, you could swim across without a guardian. Now the big boats necessitate a couple of kayaks or canoes, one on either side. I'm always one of the swimmers, but not this year. The water's cold from so much rain and I'm not sure I have that much strength yet. With only Kelly's family here at the moment, it was a small crossing, but we did uphold the tradition, plus the cherry pie afterward. Josh wore my hilarious, ruffled cancer swim cap.

Being in this normal life, with its usual frustrations and joys, is a bit hard after this winter. I go along playing jacks with my granddaughter Abby, building a fire, planning how to feed this brood, and I forget the cancer for a while. When it comes back to me, it's a surprise all over again, a sinking. A gloom settles in and only gradually moves to the back shelf of my mind.

Everything's the same here, as it has been at our cottage for 96 years. But nothing is the same because there never *was* a "same." Here are the ghosts of my great-grandparents, my grandparents, my parents, floating all over the place. There's running water now, but there's also in my mind the well, the pump. There's the old dock on sawhorses as well as the new, wide one on metal brackets.

There's the old kitchen with the washtubs and the new one with a double sink. The old life is simultaneous with the new one in my mind, one as real as the other and both of them speaking in some way to each other.

The mind makes the world. So what will my grandchildren see? I think more about my mortality, of course, of what they'll remember, how my ghost might be a benefit to them in some way, as my Grandmother Brown's been for me. Her ashes are still here, but it's her living presence in my mind that matters. I can almost hear her voice.

I never forget how incredibly fortunate I am to have my childhood intact in these woods, in this cottage. There's a Spanish word, *querencia,* I found in *Christopher Columbus and the Conquest of Paradise* by Kirkpatrick Sale (I highly recommend it). According to Sale, it means much more than "love of home." It means "a deep, quiet sense of inner well-being that comes from knowing a particular place of the earth, its diurnal and seasonal patterns, its fruits and scents, its history and its part in your history and your family's." When you're there, your soul gives a sigh of recognition and relaxation. Your compass points directly down. Columbus didn't have that, apparently. He spent his life wandering. I do have it. This is my place. When I'm here, my body's perfectly aligned with the universe.

Oddly, even though I have those sinking times, at the same time I feel a part of an ongoing movement, generation to generation and shifting of one tradition into another, a sense of being relaxed into that movement and content to have/have had my part in it. My hunch is, I still have a number of good years. I could be wrong. But it feels as if my absence will be more like another shifting of things, like getting electric lights in place of the old kerosene lamps. Eventually the cottage will need to be torn down, maybe another one built. Eventually all this will be forgotten. But it will still be there, simultaneous with the new, in some way I can't understand with my mind, in the way everything is here at the same time, influencing and informing what we call the present.

35   Smile at the Camera

I HAD A GOOD walk yesterday through cornfield stubble. I like staying off pavement—it saves my knees. But do not think the stubble resembles the top of my head! The top of my head is a finer texture, and shorter by far. It's been 50 days since my last chemo, not quite two months. I've watched the "hair regrowth after chemo" videos—cute young women smilingly displaying each month's growth. "You can generally expect to regrow an inch of hair about two months after you stop treatment, followed by a full head of hair within six months to a year," says one site. Nonsense. I think the variation has to do with the length and duration of chemo and radiation. Mine was long. And, too, the kind of chemicals. I read there's one that can cause permanent hair loss (not the one I had). And my age. Hair is thicker and more abundant when you're young.

I admit, I'm obsessed with this, especially now that I can hope to be Normal Again. Every morning I study what's in the mirror to see if I can tell the difference from the day before. The pale strands are all wacky, some barely showing above the skin, some sticking up and turned every which way. My friend Judith says it's like a dandelion gone to seed. Or, I'd say it's like a symphony tuning up, each instrument testing itself randomly, by itself, not at all playing in concert yet. You wouldn't want to listen to that for more than a minute.

There was a woman in her late 80s getting her chemo at the same time I did. She had long white hair, quite elegant. I thought her hair would never fall out. But then great clumps were missing, more each time I saw her. Why didn't she cut it off? I thought maybe at her age, her hair had been long for so many years she couldn't bear the cutting. Or, she was too old to notice how much was gone. She wound what was left around her head until it was a lost cause. The last time I saw her, she was wearing a knit beanie, but then switched, laughing, to a short, curly blonde wig when she left the office.

What strikes me is how we all smile at the camera, smile at whoever's looking, as if we're too self-confident to let a little thing like hair loss slow us down. It does help, I admit, to project that face. As one woman on one website said—she'd lost a lot of hair permanently—"If this is the price for not dying of cancer, then okay."

I'm struck by the ferocity of the body and mind as it turns toward wellness. During all that awful (I will say that now) treatment, there's a hunkering down, an enduring. But then comes a dramatically strong impetus toward wellness, the mind and body fighting their way back. I haven't wanted to use the metaphor of "fighting," as in "fighting this cancer." But NOW it feels absolutely right. I can feel every hurt, damaged cell flexing its little muscles. I am flexing my muscles. Something in me is more aggressive than previously. I wouldn't call it anger—at least it doesn't feel that way. Just insistent, assertive.

There is a field of thistles in bloom, across the road from our cottage. I can now walk two miles without tiring too much. If I do that, I don't feel like swimming, too. One or the other. Yesterday I walked the two miles and Jerry and I went for a canoe ride after supper. The water was beautiful and I wanted to swim, but I was done for the day.

I got 25 advance copies of my new book of poems last week. I do think it's my best so far. I like thinking that. I wonder if the next one will be as good, if my brain's had too much chemo to think straight. The poems I'm writing now, many of them, feel as if they suffer from not enough concentration. But I'm not sure. I seem to be "trying" less. What does that mean? I've always been stumbling in the dark with this work, anyhow.

My daughter and her family were here when the books arrived. So I got to give each of the grandchildren a copy and read a few poems to them in front of the fireplace. The book is dedicated to my grandchildren and has a series called "The Grandmother Sonnets," one about each of our ten grandchildren. Those took some explaining, since they're "adult" poems that deal with complex emotions, often alluding to difficult situations, often from my own past. Maybe they're my anti-Hallmark poems. I've always wanted to wash the sugar off my hands when I read poems by grandmothers about their grandchildren.

And the children are video-and-Harry Potter kids, not poetry kids. Reading a poem is a skill that has to be developed. They did say it helped to hear me read. Well, true for all of us. But Abby buried her head in her mother's lap and said it was too much like being in school. Sorry, Abby.

36   Cranking Up

IT'S BEEN A COOL summer, for the most part. We've spent a number of evenings in front of the fireplace in the big cottage—at one time six grandchildren, their parents, and Jerry and I.

It was on one of those fireplace nights that I screwed up my courage for that reading of "The Grandmother Sonnets." The grandchildren are ages 9-20. What a range! I could (1) hand the parents the books and trust that when the kids are older, they'll read the poems and be able to understand them, or (2) read the poems to them now and talk them through a bit and hope for the best. I showed the poems to the parents first, to get their sense of things. Then with great trepidation, I read each child his or her poem, aloud to the group, plus a few others. I warned the kids that these are adult poems. I briefly talked about what an Italian sonnet is. The parents are all big readers, but not of poetry, so I felt I needed to help them, too.

But *how much help?* If I paraphrase the poem, the poem disappears. Anyway, I don't have a nice, neat paraphrase in my head. If I did, I might as well write an essay instead of a poem. This is a bigger issue than what to do for my immediate family. Teachers have this to face all the time. Shall I give my students essentially a Cliff Notes version of Shakespeare? Shall I paraphrase for them, line by line, Hopkins' "The Windhover"?

I can't say how this all went. It was definitely most successful with the oldest children. And I told you how Abby reacted. But I figure, each child got to hear me read a poem about his or her very own self. They got to have a copy of the book. And if the words didn't make sense, the sound may imbed itself, and years later, this poem and the others might possibly carry their weight and loving attention into whatever present there is at the time.

Speaking of the present, I feel better all the time. I'm swimming my old usual route to the yellow boathouse and back, but not as often as I used to. I get cold very easily. I wear more clothes than anyone. I've achieved my professed summer goal—been out on my paddleboard. Wearing a Speedo cap, not the silly cancer swim cap I ordered.

Interlude: The paddleboard. You're standing exactly in its middle, balancing, the long pole of the paddle dipping and rising. You're Queen of the Nile. The lake is yours. Boats can roar by, testing your balancing skill, but the lake belongs to you, you and it in perfect sync, flowing with each other.

But now I'm cranking up for fall. I have two students to work with this year in the low-residency MFA program I teach in. It's a light load—students who are at a stage that requires fewer mailings. I've also made hotel reservations for the Associated Writing Program's conference in Seattle in late February. No plane reservations yet—I still might decide not to go. (My book comes out this year, and so I *should* be there.) There are other trips we will want to take. Frankly, I'm a bit scared of all that. I still feel too tired. So none if it may happen. And Jerry may have back surgery. We'll know something about that in September.

I can now pinch a little hair between my fingers. There's a widow's peak of dark on top, with white at the sides. A lot of white. All earned.

37 Here's to Negative Capability

FOG THIS MORNING. I love the lake as we move toward fall. Fewer boats, calmer water, and the water has a late-summer warmth. Swimming is better than ever for those of us who still actually do that. There's a softness in the water and air, a glow.

We're having the guest cottage and the porches on the big cottage painted. At the moment, there's wild hammering as the painters remove the old wood box from the side of the guest cottage where we live. We've cleaned out most of the remnants of my father's tenure: messy oil rags, funnels and cans, old cotton sails, rotten ropes, and now the wood-box. There's a poignancy here. The change of seasons, of administration (me, now), of what's necessary to live the life we now lead. The old water buckets and tea kettles are on the upstairs shelf of the big cottage like museum objects, no longer used. But, I should mention, the outhouse is still available.

You can actually see the passage of time here. See transition. When my cancer and its wicked potential flashes upon my inward eye (as Wordsworth would have put it), for a few minutes, I feel pretty dark. Who would want to leave this world? I'm having a good time, now that I feel better. My gut is settling down a little all the time, although I don't do well if I eat a large meal and have a sweet dessert late in the evening. I can go some days without a nap, as long as I don't swim and walk in the same day.

Another view of transition: I ran out of reading material and rummaged around here among the books Jerry brought from his office when he retired. I picked up Elizabeth Gaskell's *North and South* (Jerry specialized in the history of the novel, and especially early women novelists). Aside from the usual nineteenth-century swoons, gasps, and weeping, this is a splendid book that closely examines the worker/employer tensions in the rising industrial north of England and the tension between that world and the genteel south.

What's lost when people focus intensely on gain, on achievement? I can tell you, I lost a lot of my children's growing up. What's lost when people live more slowly, sit and talk and watch generation after generation pass with little change? Gaskell has characters speak for each side so convincingly that it's hard to see the issue dogmatically. We're left with only the thought that each "side" needs to get to know the other, to avoid destroying each other.

Feels like a contemporary issue to me. It's far more complicated than who's "right." We could use a little of Keats' Negative Capability: "when man is capable of being in uncertainties, mysteries, doubts, without any irritable reaching after fact & reason."

I'll "always" have the uncertainty of whether cancer is still lurking in me or is all gone. Neither position, "Oh, I'm sure it's gone," or "Oh Lord, it could come back at any moment" is verifiable or necessarily true. I have no idea. The mind may lean one way or the other, but basically, we have to keep on keeping on, speaking and acting, even though our words and acts are a ruffling of the seamless and timeless reality.

38 Stubbed Toe

OUR COTTAGE IS ON the east side of the lake, with a lot of big trees, so it takes the sun a long time to hit us. Yesterday, sun reflected pink off the clouds, the clouds reflected in the lake. All this reflected in my eyes, which got in a sense reflected by my brain into concepts, language.

Reflection is from Late Latin *reflexionem* "a reflection," literally "a bending back." The lake allows a bending back, even when it's wavy. To look into it awhile is to look back at your thoughts.

And *reflex,* what happens without thinking about it much. A natural, one might say original, movement of body and mind.

So, I was working on a poem which was "about" my birthday. I started it last winter, and thought to save the draft until my actual birthday this summer, to see what else I might want to do with it. I'd been reading Albert Goldbarth, which always encourages my dumping a lot of interesting but seemingly unrelated stuff into the works to see how it will all come out. I looked up the day of my birth. I put in the failure of the German Resistance, the 7,000 Jews arrested, the 1200 sent on a death march, my father in the Philippines drinking from a cocoanut that fell and broke open, his silly letters home. Then coming forward, I put the first moon landing. And my birthday parties here at the lake. And last year, when I didn't yet know I had cancer. That fact, of course, lands in any poem like a bomb.

It's not the material that makes a poem. We all know that. I gave my draft to my two best intrepid readers, who both told me, "Lovely language, but I think it's a prose poem." I thought about why they said that, which brought me to the ticklish issue of what makes a poem a poem, and not prose, or a prose poem. It's not line breaks. I had those. It's not lovely language. Apparently I'd achieved that. It's not a clear thread of meaning. A law brief does that.

Poetry, we ought to know if we don't, is a way of seeing. It can't be faked (although many try) and it can't be willed or wiled into being. But I'm pretty sure it can be driven into being by failure. We stub our toe enough times against the words, the feeling we had when we wrote the words, and a singing comes out. It may be a song of pain, but at least it'll be a song.

This is good advice for me. I'm glad I just wrote that. I look back at this draft I have to the side of me here and see that whatever elemental thing drove me to write about my birthday is still hiding behind cleverness and facts. Why did I start this poem? Because I was in the middle of chemo, or radiation, probably, and wouldn't that make you reflective about your birthdays? Wouldn't it make your heart hurt but not want to reflect that, because you have to be brave just now?

Poor Jerry has seen me come down for lunch many times after a morning of working, my head hanging in despair, my mood sour with failure. I'm used to failure. I've been a writer for a lot of years. The act of writing itself is a persistent failure to accurately reflect what we feel and see and know in the heart. Because understanding has no language. As soon as we impress language upon that understanding, we've broken it apart. All language can do is point in the direction of understanding.

I won't show you these sad drafts because that seems to harden them into place. Why am I writing this and not working on the poem? Good question. Maybe it's part of the mysterious process of writing the poem. Or maybe I'm ducking the hard work.

My little desk at the cottage does not face a window. The lake's too pretty out there. I need to use the wall in front of me as a lake, let it bend back to me my own hopeless thoughts until something emerges I can work with.

39 Threshold

LAST DECEMBER I WROTE, "The moment I heard the word cancer, I could feel myself cross a threshold, on the side now of those who know they'll die." I'm reporting to you, after nine months, including a lovely summer, that it IS a threshold. One can't cross back over it.

Recently I ran across a poem, "Ariel View," by Chicago poet Debra Bruce (who's also had cancer) that gets at this. It begins:

Shot from her life not once but twice,
she slips her healthy body back on but can't quite fit
among those friends snug in their skins
who marvel in murmurs at her return,
who think that after such a flight, her drink
will always be spiked.

Bonk anyone on the head with the fact of her mortality and she's going to wake up to her life, to some extent! She's going to become loosened from what seemed so immediate and crucial before. And she's also going to be newly and sharply aware that she can't control things.

I suppose one reaction to that knowledge may be a greater desire to control—more visits to the doctor/herbalist/acupuncturist, etc., an obsessive concern with food and exercise, a renewed devotion to religious practice and ritual, for example. Not that these aren't all worthy and helpful. The operative word is "obsessive."

Another reaction might be a greater relaxation into the moment: this is my life. It's what I have, now. I never had anything more than that, but now I see it. Wally likes this idea.

In any case, there does seem to be a separation, a distance between "me" and those who've not yet seen their mortality staring them in the face, and also between "me" and my everyday passions, my desires, my joys and my sorrows. They're all there, but I don't seem to live inside them the way I used to.

Recently I had a little scare, what I thought was a possible sign of something amiss. Apparently not—my doctor even had me take a stool sample to make sure—but in those few hours before I began to relax the fear, I imagined all the way out to the end: my death. At each step, it was only what it was—not any overarching concept or ideas about death, which might scare me to death—but only a step-by-step letting go. When I got to the last step, it was only a cessation of breathing. This was useful. Honestly. I seem to have relaxed a bit since then.

We're having, I think, the last of the summer-like warmth. Yesterday I took out the kayak, had a long swim, and Jerry and I had a beautiful canoe ride. I spent a while on the end of the dock with a book. I'm reading Jim Harrison's *True North*, set mostly in Michigan's Upper Peninsula. I'm enjoying "being in" the places we visited last fall on our first trip Up North.

40 The Edge of What We Know

MY FEW GLORIOUS DAYS alone at the lake are winding down. This is the time of year that I try to beat my record on "last swim of the season." The problem is that I don't stay at the lake quite as long as it would be possible to swim. Sunday the air was 53 degrees, the water 64 when I went in. It was actually lovely, if gray, and after a couple of minutes it started sprinkling. By the time I headed back, it was raining pretty much, the drops hitting the water and bouncing so that from water level, it looked like bubble-needles bouncing off the surface. Very lively and random. An amazing perspective.

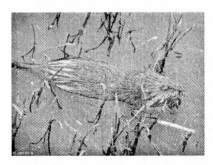 Yesterday was gorgeous, water almost perfectly still, the water 67 and the air 60. How could I NOT swim? While I was sitting on the dock, that darn little muskrat swam right under me, the one that's eaten every single one of the water reeds down by the kayaks. And digging deep holes beside a couple of trees. What can I do? He seems to be sure he wants to live here, and I'm not about to assert my dominance by killing him.

Friday is my first check-up appointment with my oncologist. Notice how I just slip this in here. Just the sight of him makes me nervous, but I expect this to go fine. If trouble develops, my guess is that it will take more time. But I feel as confident as possible, considering. I'm not sure if he'll send me for a scan or what.

A book arrived today, critical essays about poetry. I like to keep up with anything that might help my MFA students, and also I like to keep up with current conversations among poets. But I have to say, I'm tired of essays that tell me over and over that there's no way to talk about or even think about poetry, because the truth of it falls in the cracks between language. There's something to that, but the job of the critic is to offer help! Not this one.

Poets/fictionists are liars. They make things up as they go along. Given. Language can never tell the whole "truth." Given. French critics of the past 20 years reminded us that language has no intrinsic meaning: the reader makes up the stories in a negotiation between mind and page. Putting this in Buddhist terms, I'd say "Yes, sure. But talk to me about how to see what's in front of my face. Eventually I'll reach the limits of language and see for myself that what I write or read isn't the whole story. Nothing to do but stop there and imagine on out beyond."

41   Spiritual

MY LAST SWIM THIS year was at 7:15 p.m. last Thursday, water temp. 68, air 70. It was such a beautiful evening that even though I'd taken a fairly long walk with my uncle that afternoon, I decided to swim. It was supposed to rain on Friday, and I had to pack up and leave, anyway.

It's easier to leave in bad weather. It did rain. But it's no fun to go in and out to the car with coolers, blender, food processor, boxes of food, clothes, clothes on hangers, my 10 lb. weights, lawn chairs to repair over the winter, wicker rocking chair to take to the re-weaver, computer, printer—pretty much like a real move.

Too much, maybe—walking, swimming, and packing up, carrying stuff out and then up stairs into our house—I'm having arthritic-type stiffness and pains in my hips and knees. A new thing for me. Every shift of my body, every pain, I register in a new way—what does it mean? My oncologist told me that most cancer recurrences reveal themselves in symptoms, not in scans and exams. My first exam after chemo, by the way, was Friday afternoon. All's well, but I expected as much. It's too soon, probably, for trouble. It would take a while for a stray cancer cell to begin to do its dirty work.

But I'm not thinking much about this. I'm living my life, as instructed by my oncologist. As far as the hip and knee pain, my guess is my body's been generally damaged by the abuse of chemo and radiation, and it may be effectively "older" than it was. And then, I AM older. I had my 69th birthday this summer.

My oncologist says you measure success of treatment in two ways: (1) look in the mirror; and (2) birthdays.

Demarcations lead to assessments, it seems. I see that my dedication to writing has taken on more of a spiritual dimension, or, rather, I guess I'm more clear about that dimension. I dislike the word *spiritual.* What in the world does it mean? What I mean is that I seem to have a new and intimate kinship with my forebears in this practice of writing, and—in a way I can't fully understand—I'm more sure that this daily trying to say what can't exactly be said is noble, soul-saving and soul-wrenching work, not to be apologized for, taken lightly, or distorted by a lust for fame.

It is as crucial as—and maybe identical to—the nun's prayer, the priest's vow.

Your next question might be "How does your Buddhist practice fit into this?" I started the practice, as do most people, because I was anxious, God knows. I was on the verge of leaving my second marriage. I wanted some peace, meaning at that time, I suppose, escape. It didn't take long for me to see that the escape route is *into,* not *out of.* Well, out of the marriage, but into my hoard of suffering. I meditate daily. It seems that the more aware I am of how things actually are, the more true even my words can be.

When I was a teenager, I thought for a while I wanted to be a minister. What I wanted, I think—looking at it from this distance—was to lift myself up, to float above this difficult, mundane world. I think of *Madame Bovary.* Like Emma, I wanted romance in my life, any kind I could get. That was part of it. It took me years to see that what I really wanted was to live a real life. To be intimate with what's real. And then somehow to find words for that intimacy. Looks as if I'm the same person I've always been. Or, I'm like a snowball, getting fatter with my past clinging to me as I roll downhill.

Roll? A subtle Wobbly Bicycle allusion?

42   Just a Way of Talking

I DEFINITELY HAVE AN increasing sense of the sacred nature—I'll call it that—of this work of the imagination, fiction and poetry. My friend Ann Pancake had a splendid essay in the *The Georgia Review* on this very subject. Ann is talking about her choice to fictionalize the awful destruction of land and culture caused by mountain-top mining in her home state of West Virginia (and elsewhere). Documentation would have been one response. But what if you get down inside, if you imagine what it's like?

Literature, she says, both the reading and the writing of it, reunites our conscious and unconscious mind. This, she says, is imperative. Our culture has elevated the conscious to the "complete neglect, if not outright derision of the unconscious. This is disastrous not only because such psychic amputation cripples people, contributing to feelings of emptiness, insatiability, depression, and anxiety, but also because within that castoff unconscious—in intuition, in dreams—dwell ideas, solutions, and utterly fresh ways of perceiving and understanding."

"I know my unconscious is eons ahead of my intellect," she says, "worlds larger in vision than my rational mind." Artists, she says, are translators between the visible and invisible worlds, intermediaries between the profane and the sacred. Only by desacralizing the world, over centuries, have we given ourselves permission to destroy it.

I'm thinking the intellect is like a sailboat. Here I am, back at the sailboat-as-metaphor. It wants to move from point A to point B. It

calculates the wind direction and reefs or lets out its sails according-
ingly. It feels pretty proud of itself, getting from point A to point
B. But it is entirely beholden to the water and the wind, what I'll
call the unconscious mind. The two minds together do the work.
Neither can feel too arrogant.

That analogy is all wrong. Both minds are one mind, and the idea
of "mind" is itself just a way of talking. What IS the mind? Where
are these "parts" of it?

Whoa, you might be thinking, where's cancer in all this? Are you
going to abandon that subject now? But I tell you, if you've had
Stage 3C cancer, the subject is never abandoned. It becomes part of
the point of view, henceforth. (H2O + cancer) = the water I sail in.
Everything is the water we swim in—this fall day, the impending
disaster in this country brought to us by *not* seeing how connected
we all are. Etcetera.

I don't mean to say that the "point" of writing poems or fiction
is to make us feel empathy. It's not to make us do anything. Ann
Pancake's novel, *Strange as This Weather Has Been,* is not a polemic,
not even a gentle sermon. We take its characters and their lives into
us. We never get rid of our new awareness that these people are like
us, are us.

One of the interesting things about (good, rich) poetry is the way
it requires our full participation. There are those gaps that can't be
filled by explication or paraphrase. We know that when we read it.
We're both exhilarated and frustrated. We can neither agree nor
disagree with the poem. We step into a space where the intellect
loses its bearings. We move into it not knowing, but knowing, in
some way, where we are.

Cancer moves into my poems, many times not visible, not para-
phrasable, but felt.

What else? I did too much, it seems, the last week at the lake. Showing off to myself, probably. I now have what appears to be sciatica.

My left hip hurts! I checked with my oncologist's nurse to see if she thought chemo played any part in this. She said no. I'm headed now to PT.

43   A Village

WHEN I WAS VERY young, my hair was blonde and wildly curly. When it began to darken and straighten, my Nana—and my mother, I guess, but she'd go along with anything my Nana said—would send me up the street to the old ladies' beauty shop to get a perm. I would come home, stand weeping in front of the mirror, wet the bangs, and try to pull the curl out. Later, my mother administered the dreaded Toni Home Permanent with awful regularity. I wanted to look like Twiggy. I wanted straight, boyish hair. I have always pinned a lot on the connection between who I want to be and my hair.

At the moment, I can pinch my "bangs" between thumb and forefinger. Not much, but it's coming along. Upside: my hair may grow slowly, but it's thick, as thick as it always was, it seems. It's steely gray, coming to a point of gray at the front, whiter on the sides. Patchwork. The lower back is darker gray, the crown and upper back are lighter gray. As it gets longer, the unevenness doesn't seem so radical. I do not tire of this analysis. A once-in-a-lifetime (one fervently hopes) chance to see what's under there, like tracing my own development, hairless baby to eventual full head.

It seems as if I'm slowly watching myself come back together. I am having cataract surgery tomorrow. When you've had surgery for detached retina and a vitrectomy, the lens of the eye develops a cataract very quickly. My right eye is all foggy. When this surgery is over, it'll be as clear and see as well as in its original state, before nearsightedness set in.

Eventually we'll all be in our original state, if you want to go that far! Dust to dust. I'll settle for the original I can imagine, being what's called *well*, all systems working.

Evidence: I just launched my new book. A cake, guitar and singing, the whole shebang. Of course I cried, just looking out at so many people who've supported me through my chemo and radiation. I felt, then and now, surrounded by love, and simultaneously intensely aware of those who have to endure that godawful treatment with few friends and not-enough love.

I know. I had few friends all the way through school. Usually one at a time, someone to hang onto on the rocking boat. When my children were small and I was barely holding back the inward-collapsing walls of my marriage, and I hadn't figured out what to do with my young life, wasn't yet teaching, what was I doing? Staring out the window. Lonely as hell. Snapshot, again: Gray skies. Winter. No one to talk to. A haze in my mind. There've been other times, later, when I've been that lonely. I honestly do think, as Hilary Clinton wrote, it does take a village. It takes a village to raise children without trapping them within your own narrow prejudices; it takes a village to disperse some of the fear and anguish of a terrible diagnosis. To let some others help you carry it. Most likely this is why I'm writing this.

44   PTSD, Redux

I WENT TO THE dentist on Monday for a regular checkup. My teeth are always exemplary. I haven't had a cavity in, what, maybe fifteen or twenty years. It's just a matter of cleaning and polishing. This time the hygienist's pic caught in a soft spot. She had the dentist check it. Yeah, a small bit of decay starting under an old crown.

What was interesting was my reaction. I had a mini-version of the moment in the oncologist's office when he told us of the severity of my cancer. A soft blankness, a backing off of the mind. A momentary floating sensation. Life is going on, people are talking, this is about me, I know that, I know there'll be consequences to what's being said, but no one can cry at this point, just take the language that's coming my way.

It took about ten minutes to numb my jaw and fill the cavity. No big deal.

I'd gone in feeling fine, a little proud of myself for having good teeth, but surprise! Not quite as I thought it would be. I think that's what triggered the reaction. I thought I was in great health, too, when I got my diagnosis. Then, I thought it would be a little, minor sort of cancer. We'll take care of this as fast as possible and I'll be fine. Then. No. A big scary cancer. Nothing, nothing was the way I thought.

I was the one of the three sisters who was going to live to a ripe old age. I was the strongest and healthiest. I could take care of them, even, being the oldest. I would surely be able to take care of Jerry.

We all seemed to agree on this. A good lesson in presumptions. We only see the trunk and foliage of a tree. Most of it's underground.

Another late symptom: I'm clenching and grinding my teeth at night. And I am waking and lying awake sometimes, needing to take some Melatonin to get back to sleep. I've always been a great sleeper. Hit the pillow, wake up and it's morning. Last night I slept fine. The night before, not. No particular reason for one or the other that I can see. I got fitted for a bite splint to wear at night.

Here's an analogy: you have a major oil spill in the ocean. The huge vacuum machines move in, barrier bars are set in place, the beach is skimmed off, wildlife washed. Millions of dollars are spent. After a while, you can hardly tell there was a spill. But in the water, miniscule droplets of oil. Things aren't really the same. The subtle damage begins to show itself.

What I might call a deeper level of psychological damage is beginning to show itself. I called it PTSD earlier. This is the more elusive form, coming on now, it seems, working toward the surface so it can be seen. The good news is that it's working into my awareness. I can imagine, instead, dodging invisible bullets like a soldier returned from Afghanistan.

Too, I still get so tired. It's been four months since my last chemo. I know I expect too much, but I hate having to spend a chunk of the afternoon taking a nap. If I have too many appointments in one day, I'm bushed. I am not "normal." Not yet and maybe not ever, completely.

Normal? What is this "normal," Kimosabe? What was ever "normal"? In my life, in my mind. I am not what I once thought I was. I never was what I thought I was. Was I a bad mother? A good one? Probably both. Was I a good wife? I was always there, cooking what he liked, fishing if he wanted to do that, staying up late watching movies if he liked that, bringing him a heating pad, coffee, Cokes, getting up early to get the kids off for school so as not to wake him. Which husband am I talking about? Either or both.

I argued with him fiercely, tried valiantly to make him into what he could never be, then turned away in disgust. Disappeared him when he was right there in front of me. This was easy for me. I learned it growing up. When things are too hard, you don't have to look at them. Scott, also, tried very hard not to see, not to remember. He has trouble remembering things to this day.

Let's see—which husband was I describing? Either or both.

In the present, I love being alive. It's good. I'm writing, enjoying my friends, thinking about Jerry's upcoming back surgery, carrying my own future like a vague cloud over my head, getting a bite splint, going for walks, kicking fall leaves. Some days are sunny and warmish, some not.

45   Love & Death

DID SOMETHING IN ME know, when I titled my new poetry collection *No Need of Sympathy,* that I was in danger already? But consider: most poetry is about love and death. Okay, I'm not dead. But the very word *cancer* sounds the echo of mortality.

It always comes down to that, love and death. We almost can't help ourselves from slowing down or stopping at a car crash, even when we can be of no use there. We're looking for something we probably won't find until the moment of our own death. A clarity, a sense of what this life is, at its root.

Love: the same. I start a poem by loving a leaf, or a vase, or a moment, an emotion of the moment. But, oh, what if I can't hold on to it? The more love, the more sense of what its absence feels like. If I stay with the beloved without flinching, it leads me to where love and loss, love and death, are interchangeable. Don't ask me what that means. It just feels that way.

Is Keats's sonnet, "When I Have Fears" bleak? It seems to me that the only way a poem can qualify as bleak is when it doesn't touch bottom, when it doesn't reach the place where love and death merge in some sort of glorious jazz, some bow scraping across catgut, some brush-stroke made of a perfect balance of pushing and pulling.

Paradox is the only way there is to speak of anything real. Not this, not this, but something that requires the two.

Of course. Those of us who write poems are fervently hoping for the tone, the language, the pull toward death and the pull toward life to be in perfect balance to sound the music of the spheres. I think it's what we do, all of us in our own way, with whatever art, in this precious time we have before our own personal gravitational collapse.

46   What We Get From Each Other

HOW IS IT WE rub off on each other? If you're a writer, like me, you read every poem, every story, with two minds. First the enjoying mind. Second, the "what can I get out of this" mind. Same when we're with, in person, people we admire. My first year at the University of Delaware, while I was still teaching part-time and finishing my grad work at Arkansas, Sir Angus Wilson was Delaware's distinguished writer-in-residence. I could have taken Angus's course, but I didn't. I think I was afraid of making a fool of myself.

The great poet James Wright spent a semester at Delaware the year before he died. Dennis and I, and the kids, took a long walk in the woods together with his wife Annie and some friends. I remember his singing Scott the French Chef's song from Sesame Street and showing him the burls on trees, explaining how they were made. No one talked about writing.

I've rubbed shoulders with many writers while I was at Delaware. What is it, what do we get from each others' presence? When I was younger, I thought it was a game of who knows stuff and who doesn't. But I'm certain now that it isn't the exchange of information that matters, it's the *presence* of one whose life has been utterly given over to, to, to *something*—to expression, to art, to seeing, to knowing, I don't know what to call it, but I know it when I see it, the face of complete abandonment, not just abandonment, but abandonment TO something. To something worth everything.

The late poet Larry Levis, for example. He's like Elvis to me. A true artist. Given over entirely.

A comment from another great, Jim Harrison: "Though I don't teach I often get sought for advice from young poets. I say I don't have time for you unless you're going to give your life to it. That's what it takes."

Which brings me back to my question, have I been a good mother? When the kids were very young, I was walking, talking, cooking, and giving baths through a fog of dissatisfaction. When I was able to go back to graduate school, I was in a fog of study. The fogs combined, escalated toward the Ph.D. I began writing more poems. They started getting taken by journals. It was as if all the pins finally fit into the lock, and I was, without thinking about it at all, giving my life to this work.

People said, "You're a good mother." But I knew better. My mind was never clear. My heart was bleeding. Just like my own parents, I tried my best, and whatever flawed love I could give, I gave. Guilt. What we carry. Scott told me years later that he and a friend had written down a list of dirty words, given each of them a number and gone around school calling people the numbers. One of his teachers confronted him and made him give her the list. She wrote a letter for him to take home to me, but he couldn't show it to me. So he buried it in the back yard, lived in dread for weeks that I would somehow discover it.

Do these moments knot up in us and make us sick? I don't have a clue.

47   My Letter to the World

THERE ARE BOOKS, LIKE this one, and there are letters, the smaller, more immediate ways we rub off on each other. The actual, physical presence of letters. I am supremely glad to have Keats' letters. Hemingway's. Even T. S. Eliot's. Soon there'll be no letters from writers to illuminate their work, their thoughts about it and about other writers, and their lives. Saul Bellow's letters were published a couple of years ago, William Styron's last year. Maybe these are the dying gasps.

I was reading a book review by Mason Currey in the *New York Times*. He's more concerned with what the dearth of letter-writing is doing, not to its faithful followers and researchers, but to creative writing itself. He says "Letters were not only a way to stay in touch with colleagues or test out ideas and themes on the page, but also a valuable method of easing into and out of a state of mind where they could pursue more daunting and in-depth writing."

I think lately the blog is covering some of the same territory. Emails aren't. I use emails for transactions, mostly. I use them to invite people for dinner! Email protects me. I like people, I hasten to say, but I need space between connections. Space is both empty and like an *ahem*. Clearing the throat. I often tell students that they need to cut the first stanza, or the first few paragraphs, from their work. "That's just you, warming up," I tell them. "It's served its purpose. Now you can get rid of it."

Granted, letters from one writer to another are more intimate and often more revealing than what's written for general consumption, those bloggy Letters to the World, which, interestingly enough, is how Emily Dickinson begins one of her typically intimate poems. ("This is my letter to the world.") If you know you're being read by a lot of people, many of whom you don't know, you change registers. You're on stage. This is the loss from the lack of letter-writing. What we gain is "letters" from a whole lot of quite good writers that we might never have gotten to read in our lifetime.

Nothing has mattered more to me during my chemo and radiation this year than getting something regularly written. There are so many therapeutic reasons, of course, why that might have been true, but beyond that, actually the cancer was just another subject, one of burning interest to me. How is that different from what I've been doing all my writing life—coming to whatever burning interest presented itself to see how it might work itself out in words?

48   Doctors, Ad Seriatim

TODAY WE'RE HEADING DOWNSTATE, to Ann Arbor, having a pre-op consultation for Jerry's very-big-deal back surgery on December 3. He'll be in the hospital for about a week, rehab after that. About six months' recovery time. Another winter of hunkering down and getting better.

How will this be for us, after last winter? A friend said she was glad to notice that cancer isn't the first thing she thinks of when she thinks of me these days. I think about it less, myself. Partly, that's because it's an integral part of my system, now. You don't describe how it is brushing your teeth because you do it every day, and unless you find you have a loose tooth, it's not worth mentioning.

Coming back from chemo and radiation is a little like returning to the world after, say, a year in a monastery. The world seems fast and energetic. I didn't realize how small it had grown last winter. I seemed to still DO things—wrote this, wrote commentaries for IPR radio, wrote some poems, had a book launch party, spent time with people as often as I could. Nonetheless, my mind was turned in on itself, the way the minds of the sick do, gathering its forces to keep on keeping on.

I still tire easily, just to say. I get overwhelmed even by being in a big store, shelves and shelves of stuff, mental noise. It's an interest-ing quality of tired. Not the old "I'm bushed" kind, the body feel-ing a bit deliciously tired, worn out from activity. It feels kind of *chemical*, I'll call it that for lack of a better description. It feels like a deep inability in the bones to muster the basic elements of aliveness. Maybe it'll always be this way. Probably I'll get some better, maybe a lot. Sometimes I'm discouraged, sometimes not. And I still have pain and weakness in my left hip from whatever overuse that must have occurred last summer, still trying to improve this with physical therapy.

So now we plunge back into the fray, negotiating the giant University of Michigan Medical Center and all that implies. Jerry worries how this will be for me. What about him? One partner doesn't have cancer, you know. It's both. Last year was difficult for him, too, and now he's in for it again, though different. One thing at a time.

Who can do more than one thing at a time? First this thing, then the next. That's how it goes. Trouble only feels Huge if I start adding into the mix all my projections and concepts about it. And when I do that—this is what my meditation teacher says—it's only a problem if I begin blaming myself for doing it! Adding, adding, adding to what was essentially one thing.

One-thing-at-a-time is the gift Trouble gives, is what I see. Not as in balancing the scales, not as in "Something good always comes out of it." There's not a sunny "side" to illness and pain, period. But I see there's a recalibration, a slowing down, a reconsideration made possible by the slowing down: what am I doing with my one precious life? Which maybe ought to be amended to *Am I even noticing my one precious life?*

49 Not Norman Rockwell

MANY OF US TRY to replicate Norman Rockwell in our own fami-
lies. You'd think that would create the same tension as Christmas
does, as it also tries to be Rockwell plus Clement Moore plus the old
Coke Santa image. But it mostly doesn't.

I love the purity of Thanksgiving. Not so much of the exchange,
the cash-nexus, that Christmas often promotes. More about the
thanks, less about the giving/getting. Lord knows I'm grateful to
have gotten through this last year. I'm grateful for my dear family,
my friends, my work, my community. I'm grateful for the history
of cancer research that has saved me from early death. I could go
on forever. I'm grateful for the snow, the birds. I'm grateful for
those who've dedicated their lives to helping others, to rescuing
the environment.

But here's something subtle that I learned from my meditation
practice: each time I recite part of that litany, I separate myself and
I separate the situation into me-and-them. I also put myself in the
center of the dynamic—all those who've given *me* something, even
secondarily. When actually, this is all a web that operates without
the need for that pushing and pulling, that "Thank YOU for what
I (also in bold) have." That expectation of gratitude or reward.

So then, how to respond? Nothing wrong with a simple "Thank
you" to the universe, but I'm thinking that the best response would
be simply my attention. To the lowliest of moments with the same
awareness and appreciation as one gives the dramatic ones.

So. . . . We'll have Thanksgiving dinner tomorrow with my sister and brother-in-law at a restaurant here in Traverse City. Millie has trouble cooking. Standing at the stove hurts her back. We decided this would be more fun than watching me do all the work. Then later, Jerry and I will visit friends in Empire for dessert. My daughter Kelly and her big family are hosting a huge dinner in Washington D.C., where they now live. My sister's children and grandchildren and my son and his family will all be in D.C. I'm sad not to be there. You should see the snow here, already this year.

We'll be on our way Sunday to Ann Arbor for Jerry's back surgery. His surgery, he reminded me this morning, is exactly five days from when I had my surgery last year. Amazing, that this winter will have some of the same flavor as the last one. Recovery. I keep being astounded at how the human spirit picks itself up, brushes itself off, and starts all over again. If you're singing along, good.

I see now how this aging thing goes, one little (or big!) thing after the other, each one a surprise, "Oh, I didn't think this would happen to ME." The mind/ body coasts on, thinking it can still manage the same things, and gradually learns that it can't, that things have changed. It adjusts to the change. We compact in the same way our old spines do, into a denser, more intense awareness of being alive. Ted Kooser was right. It may be that I enjoy being alive more than ever.

50 Out of My Hands

TODAY MARKS ONE YEAR of this writing, this wobbling. But when am I ever NOT on a wobbly bicycle? And certainly after cancer, one is evermore aware of how great it is to fly along in perfect balance. Whatever balance I have contains tentativeness, a little to this side, a little to the other.

Jerry and I are in Ann Arbor, at the University of Michigan Hospital, where he just had back surgery. If you like drama, I could mention that he was in the O.R. for ten hours, with four surgeons in attendance. It must have been interesting, to figure out how to "fix" the spine from the deformity that develops after many years of the body's leaning, trying to correct itself. Scoliosis and stenosis. The motif is balance, our wobbly-bicycle bodies.

So, knowing how huge the hospital is, I brought a trekking stick with me. I'd have to walk a lot, and here I am, having some sort of back/pinched nerve issue myself, that causes me to limp if I walk very far. (There was no time to see a specialist before we left. I did have a hip x-ray, nothing wrong with my hips.) So, anyway, I'm using the trekking stick like a cane, and it keeps me from limping, which I think is a good idea, to keep from throwing my body out of kilter.

This is all hilarious, from one perspective, the accumulation of woes. Me here, limping along. It's interesting, being a "disabled" person, getting those quick glances, that special consideration, holding elevator doors, etc. I feel like I'm faking it, but then, I suspect all disabled people feel whole inside.

This large hospital feels like a magical enclosure. I'm thinking of the people I see, *in extremis*, the nakedness of the situation. I was taking a three-legged walk down the long hallways today, and of all things, I was noticing that there's a deep pleasure that comes, no matter what the anguish, in putting aside the posing and ambition that seemed so crucial, just being glad for the nurse who comes when you ring, the ginger ale, the extra pillow.

I think it's like being at the seashore, Kelly's favorite place. It's the expanse, she says, unlike our little lake. The waves come in and go out, and you can't do anything about any of it. Even in Hurricane Sandy, you can't do anything about it, so you just act like a plain person for a change, taking care of what you can take care of, what's right in front of you to do.

I sat for a while yesterday in the interminable time before the buzzer went off telling me Jerry was out of surgery, thinking how I might write about any of this—the immediacy of it. Well, I didn't sit. I paced through corridor after corridor, studied the photos of surgeons and benefactors on the wall, examined the art objects behind glass, got things from the café, listened to the pianist in the lobby, sat in half a dozen different seats, read a little and pretended to read a lot more. It was all just there, nothing to do about it. Out of my hands. You have to just leave moments like that alone, if you're going to write about them, let them bubble up at another time, in another way.

51 Misery

"MANY YEARS LATER I understood that because of the privations and the poverty of their lives, Russians in general liked to entertain themselves with misery: they played with it like children, and they were rarely ashamed to be wretched." That's from Maxim Gorky's *Childhood*, that has just come out in a new translation. This is from the end of Chapter X. He goes on:

> "In the endless tedium of daily life, grief becomes a holiday; a fire's an entertaining show. On a blank face, even a scratch is a beauty mark."

Gorky's childhood was full of yelling, abandonment, drunkenness, beatings and more beatings, and all manner of deprivation. This was one of the books I was reading at the hospital. I would look into rooms where people lay alone or with an occasional visitor, and hooked up like Medusa to a tangle of tubes. Others sitting up in bed, surrounded by family, all watching TV and laughing together as if they were having a regular night. All varieties.

Then I started a new biography of Mozart and made note of these words: "Mozart avoided the noisy and empty fireworks that spoil so many of the violin works of the period. He thought them silly. He said he was 'no great lover of difficulties for their own sake.'"

I was thinking of how we respond to both our own pain and that of others. Sometimes it seems we're in love with difficulty for its own sake. Makes a good story afterward. The large scar, the almost-dying, the awful pain. But that's when things turn out well. No one falls in love with serious, terrible difficulty.

I'm frankly tired of talking about chemo and radiation. I'd just as soon leave it in the past. But every time I start writing anything—including what I'm still writing here—I'm on the lookout for the glitch, the place where there's not smooth sailing, where there's something to work with. Tension. You should see the line of staples down Jerry's back! Frankenstein's monster, backwards. But hooray, it looks as if he's going to be a lot better, the nerves having much more room to breathe. Rising action, climax, denouement. In short order.

I'm willing to suspend a good ending, if the details are so intriguing that I'm caught in them, living the uncertainty. I'm willing to lose myself in a character, to see deep into the life, into its inherent ambiguities. But even then I notice there's always some sort of tension and release, and I suspect that's because existence itself breathes in and breathes out. Creation and destruction are not exactly twin poles; they're simultaneous actions. When the breath sucks in, the abdomen and lungs expand. When the breath goes out, the ribs and abdomen pull inward.

I wrote my dissertation a million years ago on the American man of letters, William Dean Howells. I traced patterns of imagery in four of his best-known novels. I was interested in how a consummate realist uses images. Do they remain realistic? When do they lift off and become metaphor? I found that Howells' images alternated in an almost regular pattern from the concrete to the metaphorical/symbolic. Another example of breathing.

In Neurosurgery A corridor where Jerry was, there was in one room a bald woman who just lay there, no visitors that I ever saw. She didn't appear to move all day. I looked in as I passed one evening and saw the nurse feeding her. I will never forget the expression on the nurse's face. She didn't know anyone was watching. Her face was so full of compassion and tenderness. She could have stuffed food in the woman's mouth and daydreamed at the same time, or stared out the window. But she was giving that woman all the love she could in that moment. An absolutely bedrock realistic scene that for me lifted off into a wordless beauty.

That is difficulty and what it can draw forth. That is drama and passion. That is poetry and religion. That draws forth all the words in the world and stops all words in their tracks.

52 Sinking

JERRY'S BEEN BROUGHT BY ambulance to the rehab place. All those miles, from Ann Arbor to Traverse City in what's essentially a truck, in the ice and snow. Slow and painful going. Tonight I brought him dinner (Do you have any IDEA how badly some of our elders are fed in these places?). We watched an episode of HGTV (yes), and I cried when the man with five children whose wife had died sold his house so he could send the children to college.

Trap # 1: the word *depression*. It only confirms itself. At the moment, okay, instead I'll say the atmosphere around me is blue-black, and seems like a bass cello; no, I'd say an oboe, except that I'd see Sonia the duck in *Peter and the Wolf*. So like me, smiling at the duck while feeling like, well, shit.

Depression is a worthy word, though: a sinking. As if gravity has a double-hold. It takes longer to do everything, and I'm clumsy because of these weights attached to my spirit.

Okay, Jerry's out of surgery, I drove Wally and me home. Jerry's been at rehab over a week now, due to come home Friday. He's doing great, better than we would have imagined. Meanwhile, I have my six months' oncology checkup on Friday. My poor oncologist. He does his best to save people, and what does he get for it? Fear. As if he were the Wolf in the aforementioned Prokofiev story, fangs dripping.

I'm weary. There's been so much strain around Jerry's surgery, getting it planned, making it happen, getting to Ann Arbor, spending the week there, then home in the snow. Bringing him food. Plus several secondary health things that have had to be dealt with, one being that I'm getting a steroid shot tomorrow for the pinched nerve (yes, that's what it was) in my lumbar area. And it's a week from Christmas.

Trap #2: trying to identify a reason or reasons. If I only hadn't had to do this, or if only that hadn't happened....Who can say? Who knows what if this, or what if that?

All I'm doing is describing how I feel! I'm wondering WHEN Plath, Sexton, Snodgrass, Lowell–the poets that got stuck with the label "Confessional"—actually started those poems, if they wrote anything *in medias res*. If they did, I'll bet they woke up the next day, wadded them up and started over, with better sense.

Shall I leave these words, this evidence of my sadness? I'll probably regret it. What happens is, you're down and the mechanisms you usually use to present a face to the world collapse. So you either curl up in a corner to avoid exposure, or you say more, or different, from what you meant to.

However, Wally the Buddha cat says, "No writing is wasted." He always says the right thing. And Sonia the duck says, "What the quack? You want a good story without tension and worry and sadness? Not happening."

53 A Terrible Beauty Is Born

CHRISTMAS DAY, SNOW FALLING feathery, heaped. Deeply comforting. No sharp corners. It's stunningly beautiful and one of the reasons we live here. If I could put my skis on or even go snowshoeing, that would be nice, but there's this hip pain…. I did shovel a little, shame on me. Jerry's recuperating, so we're not going anywhere for a while. I love stopping. I love that in general, having an excuse to hibernate. I love that about poems, the way they stop. I love the lyric impulse. When there's stopping, things burst their seams.

Amy's flying in on Friday. Friends have stopped by, brought us wine, jams, cookies, little gifts, and whole meals. As I've said, 2013 has been a year of being recipients of great love and generosity. I've always been wary of sentimentality, which I think I've often translated as letting feelings show. Maybe I'd say the right thing, but the feeling of it was tamped down. Plenty of reasons in my past why that might be so, but there seems to be a softening here, now.

Heart, and how that shows up in our work, prose or poetry: I don't know. . . . I've read some effusions that meant to be heart but made me back off. As with some relationships. I'm thinking the difference is, strangely, maybe, equanimity. There's an opening, a generosity of the heart that shows up in the writing, the art, the music, that stands on its own, not leaning on anything. It doesn't say, "Oh, look at how soulful I am," or "Please love me," or "Aren't I generous?" It responds without a lot of fuss about it.

It's as if there's a vacuum that needs to be filled, so generosity moves in to fill it. The impulse has an almost impersonal quality to it. In Buddhist terms, I'd say that this is an awareness of no-separation. In Christian terms (the only two traditions I know enough about to speak), there's always Jesus between the impulse and the action.

Speaking of Jesus, whose birthday is celebrated today, Christmas sermons typically emphasize Jesus as representing hope, a new beginning, in a teleological way. A beginning (birth) and an end (death). There's a beginning (sin) and an end (redemption). The idea, generally, is to be good, generous, kind, toward some end. I prefer the sermons that talk about how we're eternally at a pivot point, always beginning again whether we're aware of it or not. And the closer we look, are we sure we know what's good and what's not? The book of Job says, more or less, "How can you possibly think you know the ways of God?"

What does openness of heart look like in art, any form of it? Here's what I'm pretty sure of: it shuts nothing out. It doesn't so much "sympathize" (feel for) as it expresses "compassion" (feeling with). That poor boy Pip in *Great Expectations,* how could Dickens have done any better at the beginning of that novel, expressing compassion? There's Pip, alone in the graveyard. It's cold, damp, foggy. He's only seven, standing among the graves of his parents and his brothers. He names them, each one.

The long first paragraph ends, "The little bundle of shivers, growing afraid of it all and beginning to cry was Pip."

Dickens can be insufferably sentimental, but not here. We are here with Pip, feeling alongside him.

And Yeats in "Easter, 1916":

I write it out in a verse—
MacDonagh and MacBride
And Connolly and Pearse

Now and in time to be,
Wherever green is worn,
Are changed, changed utterly:
A terrible beauty is born.

To memorialize is one thing. To name the names of those killed in the Easter Rising in Ireland against British rule, to bring each one to consciousness and to end with that line, "A terrible beauty is born" is about as much heart as can be expressed on paper.

In music and visual art, again, the one quality I can point to is "lack of leaning." If there is direct seeing, it isn't leaning one way or the other. If it were, there'd be blurring or distortion. Each note knows only it can speak at that moment, in concert with another, that also only knows itself. A musician might be able to explain what I mean.

This is all very psychological, what I think I'm saying. I think I know it when I see it, when the ego doesn't have top billing. When the artist is aware of what's really there, and sings what there is to sing, paints what there is to paint.

Jerry and I were listening to St. Olaf's College Choir coming from Norway. My God, what beautiful voices, what perfect sound. What struck me is how singers stand while singing, their body language. They're in identical robes, hands at their sides, relaxed, their voices carrying the whole of their individual expression. They're utterly "being with" each other and the music.

Merry Christmas, no matter what that may mean to either of us. Merry Christmas from Wally, who is fond of the Christmas tree and its dangling things, each individual one, bright and battable.

54 Going Gray

DO YOU THINK I was as cool as I said I was when my hair was all falling out into my hands? I had to say that. How else to get through it? A week ago I went for my first haircut since, what, December 2013! I regretted having even one of the precious dears trimmed, after the daily effort I've expended urging them to grow. But when hair comes back, it's like baby hair, all different lengths, which encourages wild disarray. Still, it's all curly-wild and probably will be until there's enough weight and clipped ends to settle it down. It's as thick as ever, for which I'm eternally grateful.

And then there's the issue of color. When it started going gray years ago, I started having it touched up. Gradually "touching up" became a euphemism. Still, I wanted some gray showing, a signal that I wasn't really *trying* to look young, I guess. Hair is the flag of our disposition. A signal. We say all sorts of things with it. "Keep it looking like I'm *going* gray," I told my hairdresser, who devised a technique of painting the color through, leaving strands uncolored.

But behold, here I am, my exact self in its exact color! A really nice steely gray, like my father's (he has more white now that he's 96). I've been contemplating this—gray or not gray?—for a while now. I feel good in gray. I am, after all, the age for it. My hair matches the rest of me. However, you can say all you want about gray being elegant, signaling wisdom, whatever, but basically, for those who don't yet have gray hair, aren't the gray-headed ones dismissed as somehow no longer "counting" in the contemporary whirl? I think I've felt that way.

Will I leave it gray? I have no idea. It's a joy to see at last what it really-really looks like. Remember when I said it was interesting to see my bald head—most of us (the lucky ones) go a lifetime without ever seeing what our bare scalp looks like. Color-wise, I might have kept my hair dark for a bunch more years before I gave up the illusion of a younger me. I would have, eventually—I've noticed when one is 80 or so, dark hair tends to look harsh.

For now and maybe forever, I'm liking this gray. I'm liking not wearing a wig, for sure. I've been grateful to have that absolutely perfect wig. It's made the whole chemo-radiation process much less miserable, but there's a sense of disguise. Dramatically so, with the wig, only slightly, with the color. Jerry says, "Do you feel inauthentic wearing contacts, eye makeup?" No. "So," he says, "why would you feel that way about coloring your hair?" Maybe the difference is this: cosmetics don't disguise anything; they just enhance. Color on gray hair is a disguise.

Nothing evil in that. Whatever makes us feel good when we look in the mirror is just fine in my book. I don't feel any particular nobility in choosing not to color. I read that one in six women have dyed her hair so long they can't remember its natural color. A quarter of women have their hair colored more often than cut. The hair-color aisle at the drugstore is as long as the soft drink aisle! I don't know whether I'll stay gray, but I can feel a kind of settling in my body/mind as I look in the mirror. Yes, this is me. This is me, aging. I've caught up with myself.

This is me, also, having a heck of a time getting anything written. A lot going on here, Jerry's back surgery, Christmas, Jerry's recovery routines. And so on.

I'm reading Ann Patchett's collection of essays, *This is the Story of a Happy Marriage*. She describes the unwritten novel as a glorious butterfly. You can watch it flutter for years if you wish. But to actually get it written, you have to smash the butterfly, the dream of the perfect novel, and try to build back something only somewhat like it by slogging through muck. "If you want to write," she says, "practice it for hours a day, not to come up with a story you can publish, but because you want to learn to write well, because there is something only you can say."

At this moment I'm also thinking this about the gray hair, too. There is no one else who's me.

55 Let Us Have Drifting

SNOW'S COMING DOWN TODAY at a deliberate angle, not floating like fairy-wings, so we must be moving past lake-effect into "real" snow, now that the bay is so cold. Maybe another five inches tonight. We have so little room behind our house, the snow gets dumped in a gigantic heap in the one spot. I haven't minded any of this until yesterday when there was a brief melt and we had water in great pools, then ice. But here comes more snow, covering it all up again.

That's the beauty of northern winters. I think of Jerry Dennis's gorgeous and lyrical book, *The Windward Shore: A Winter on the Great Lakes.* Here's a section: He has been listening to Bach fugues. He's describing the "mournful section" titled "Contrapuntus XIV," which ends "abruptly, shockingly, in mid-phrase." This was probably Bach's final composition, left unfinished.

> The ending is so sudden and unexpected that it resonates with significance. In the aftermath, the silence wells, leaving us like the listener in the barren winter landscape of Wallace Stevens's "The Snow Man," who "beholds /Nothing that is not there and the nothing that is." Nothing stands between us and that silence. Literally nothing. We are engulfed in the nothing, swallowed by it. The last note lingers almost more than we can bear, then recedes until it seems to blend into the eternal silence, and we are left knowing devastation and exultation in equal measures.

I just finished reading Doris Grumbach's *Fifty Days of Solitude*, a memoir of her deliberate isolation at her house in Maine. Once alone, cut off by snow, she says, "How can one not think about mortality and about why one fills up one's life with writing?" Grumbach says "I discovered that when I began to write in those dark, early mornings I approached the whole act of word choice warily. I attributed this to not wasting my verbal energies in hearing talk and in speaking. Every word I put down on paper seemed to take on a kind of holiness, a special, single precision, resembling not at all the usual detritus that was left over after spurts of talk."

Jerry Dennis says, "The more involved we become in something, the more complex is the language we invent for it."

I am not "involved." I'm scattered. I need to drive my Jerry everywhere, wait for him at PT, and look after things he normally takes care of, until his back is better. Plus, I'm aware of how much time I spend on email, how many requests, commitments, many of them small, but each one nibbling at my mind, flaking off small bits of attention. I get jittery, irritable.

This condition creeps up on me periodically until I finally get more deliberate about my life. At present, my deliberate action is to write for an hour every day in my daybook/journal, not on the computer, not poems or anything in particular, just let my mind wander on paper. To slow down. To back off from trying to accomplish anything.

White space. Snow. Test pattern (Some of us remember those), the musical rest, the line break in a poem. Not paying any particular attention. Just drifting until the next thing appears.

Last winter was focused. Do the chemo, do the radiation. Then this fall, get Jerry's surgery, look after him afterward. There's been a deficit of drifting. Let us have drifting. Let the snow fall, the sounds muffle, the sky whiten. Let the page stay blank. Let there be no need to fill it.

56 Chaos

IN ONE YEAR, LAST year, I was diagnosed with serious endometrial cancer, had chemo and radiation along with two eye surgeries, Jerry had major back surgery and is slowly recovering, still can't bend to tie his own shoes, is just now starting to drive again. And Lord, now—ta da! Announcement coming— after all my loving reference to our little house on Eighth Street, I'm here to tell you we've decided to move! Those of you who've done that know what that entails. But the opportunity presented itself. Someone badly wanted to buy our house, and we'd been looking at condos, thinking that maybe in a year or so, we might want to think about that. Not now. Later. But when things conspire in one direction, you kind of go with it.

Well, actually, we won't need to move until May, but the paperwork, the emotional disruption, is now. Which brings me to the subject for today: the kind of environment that breeds good writing. It ain't this, is my first response. But then, I remember writing while teaching, reading heaps of student papers, planning classes, sitting in committee and faculty meetings, I remember studying for my Ph.D. exams with two children still at home.

We had just moved from Arkansas to Delaware: Dennis's new appointment, teaching Journalism and English. He took the only spare bedroom in our new faculty rental house for his study. Did I have a desk? Surely so. Where was it? In the living room, I think. We were all to stay quiet so he could work. Okay, true, but I must note this in his favor: he had taken a two-volume History of American Literature and a two-volume History of British Literature and gone through all of both of them, underlining and highlighting everything he thought I needed to know. Was I his project? Yes, but he did love me, as he could. I studied, I wrote, in the interstices of this troubled life. The children made do as best they could, half my brain taken up with studying, half with keeping my anxious husband from going off the rails.

I can't say what it takes to be good at Anything. Although I do know that as far as I can see, the best writing and the best mothering has a sense of an internal quiet, no matter how noisy its surface may be.

We writers have our rituals: get the cup of tea, place it in the exact spot, the pen in the exact spot, the door shut, blinds at the right angle. That all seems fine and necessary, like a dog circling its bed before it lies down. But I do think we make too much of that imaginary control, thinking it's all about getting things *right*. "If only I got a new computer, if only the kids would be quiet, if only I didn't have to balance my bank statement. If only I were not so anxious, I could achieve enlightenment...."

We writers have our larger rituals. You could call them our religious practice. We make a commitment to sit down every day and face the page for a certain length of time. We make a commitment to read and study, to learn the tradition out of which we were formed and in which we write. We are devotees of our models, people who've done what we hope to do. Okay, but none of this is going to get work done while we're planning which of those dishes to keep, what kind of bookcases will work, what kind of new sofa we need, and how we will fit a dresser in That Spot. Things aren't going to quit being noisy for a second, no matter how many rituals I perform. If I can just live inside the chaos and not get caught by it. I enjoy it, even! What writer could exist without wading knee-deep, maybe up to the neck, in this business of living?

We will manage this. I'll tell you later about these amazing condos, the only such places either of us would willingly move to. Why do this at all? Partly because we have two very old cottages at the lake to take care of, already. Less to look after is good. No yard, no exterior maintenance. Fewer possessions (although we're going to keep two-thirds of our books!) We're also moving into a community of people, some of whom we already know.

Stupid me, stupid us, thinking of moving. You should have seen us, going to look at the condo, Jerry tooling around the kitchen leaning on his walker. Move? you'd say. These old people need to stay put in their little bungalow. Still, it's going to happen, and it seems right. Like my work: I stumble along day after day not having a clue whether what I'm doing is worth anything, is good in any sense of that word—good for the world or of good quality. I just do it because I do it. I'm pretty sure that we invent reasons after the fact.

57   Full Stop

A FRIEND WHO ALSO has had serious cancer said that since she couldn't get any writing done while she was in treatment, she organized her books. I, on the other hand, got a fair number of poems written last winter while I was in treatment. Now that I'm done, I'm unable—unwilling?—to write. I'm organizing. Everything.

The Brown family saves everything. I've been organizing boxes and boxes of love letters from my mother to my father when he was overseas during WWII, and letters from my father to his brother Richmond, and hundreds of photos taken at the cottage, and in Columbia, MO, ancestors' photos as far back as photography was available for general use.

And I've been cleaning out my personal stuff. When you make the momentous decision to move, this is what comes next. The cleaning and sorting. It's a little like planning your funeral. What do you want to be remembered by? What's important to you? Although our condo has as many square feet as our house (minus our basement), there isn't the storage space. What do I have all those files for anyway? Even on my computer, I still have the folders from when I taught full time: syllabi, lectures/lesson notes, handouts. I have a folder called "Department Business" with my letters to the Dean complaining about lack of support for Creative Writing, proposals for new hires, for lecture series, the entire history of my professional life.

Then, I have paper folders full of poet laureate archives: newspaper and magazine clippings (there were a lot, especially when I was appointed), Division of the Arts flyers about events I was involved in, posters from places where I read, and so on.

There are folders of some of the first poems I ever wrote. I've agreed to give the University of Delaware library my papers. They say they want everything, no matter how insignificant I think it is: drafts of poems, scraps with notes. They don't want me to sort. Everything I turn over to the library is theirs forever. I signed an agreement. I can visit it, but I can't remove it. That makes me hesitate. I've already given them a pile of papers, but I've balked at the earliest poems, and the poet laureate archives. What shall I keep for me and my children and what shall I give to the library? When I die, what about the rest of it?

BUT: The big question: does any of this matter? Who cares if my papers are in the library? And then I look still deeper and wonder how much the residue of an individual life matters, anyway? (I can hear Ancestry.com shouting at me!) We live our lives, wonderfully or terribly or mundanely. After we're gone, unless we were extraordinary in some way, what we leave behind matters only as long as there are those who remember. I've liked looking back through my parents' and grandparents' lives—some sadness, some nostalgia, some pleasure. Same with my life. Am I that person who did those things? Am I that person who wrote those books?

Questions like this come up, it seems, when one is at a standstill. When the wild rush toward—toward what? accumulation? recognition?—slows, or stops. When there's a suspension of evaluating, for a change. When the water in the pond settles and we can see way down toward the bottom. Is this because of the cancer? Because of our year of almost constant medical issues? Probably partly. All I know is that I'm at full stop at the moment. Not the stopping of "Oh well, I'm taking a rest." Not the stopping of "gathering my forces." Just stopped. What I'm writing here seems all I can manage.

Does this seem exaggerated, or radical? I'm not alarmed. I'm looking back at all this accumulated material, my family records, photos, my books, my file folders. It feels both warm and substantial to have these many faces and lives I've known (including my own) looking at me from some distance. And it also feels completely insubstantial.

There's no going back. There is no "back," is there? What I imagine once was, was never the way I thought it was. At the moment, I have a new book manuscript more than half done. I'll finish that in due time, unless I can't, or don't. I may write a bunch more books. Or not. Always balancing between choreographing a future and saying "whatever."

58   Art From Scraps

WE'RE MOVING IN MAY. Before, I would have said, *yuk, a condo.* Old people, shuffleboard courts. Or vacationers, a blue pool glaring from below. But this is not just any condo. I am so enamored that I want to tell you about it. I'm excited, and I haven't been much of that for awhile.

Think of our condominium as a prime example of revision. Of space, of one's life, of writing.

We're moving to a former insane asylum! Our bedroom and my study were patients' rooms. The hallways are wide to accommodate rolling carts, nurses, wheelchairs, all manner of things.

The Traverse City State Hospital was established in 1881. Lumber baron Perry Hannah petitioned to have the asylum located in Traverse City as an industry to save the town from disappearing when the trees were nearly all cut down and the lumber business was dying.

And long before drug therapy became popular in the 1950s, James Munson, the first superintendent, followed the "beauty is therapy" philosophy. Treatment for mental illness was kindness, comfort, and pleasure. Flowers were provided year-round by the asylum's own greenhouses and the variety of trees Munson had planted on the grounds. Straightjackets were forbidden.

Sixty-three acres, 27 Victorian-Italianate brick buildings, and 750,000 square feet of wooded space! Self-sustaining. They grew their own food and milked their own cows. Then the laws changed and ideas about how to treat the mentally ill changed. The hospital closed in 1989.

There were those who wanted to demolish all the buildings and put a housing development on the gorgeous grounds. But the rubble would fill all available landfills and more.

The builder, Ray Minervini, loved the craftsmanship it took to lay 11 million bricks while leaving space in three-foot-thick walls for nearly 2,000 windows. He took on the project of turning the whole thing into—what? well, condos, restaurants, a bakery, winery, galleries—a whole village, the Grand Traverse Commons. It was a huge and preposterous dream, since even re-roofing the buildings would cost millions. Nonetheless, here it is, in little Traverse City, the nation's largest restoration project. Ray's wife Marsha told us that one night she realized it was 2:00 a.m. and Ray wasn't home yet. She called his cell. "I'm just sitting here in this space," he said, "waiting for it to tell me what it wants to be."

I'm sure Ray's making money on this project, but—as is true of art, poetry, and music—it wasn't begun or carried out *for that purpose*. It was for the love of the space, to see what the space wanted to be *now, this time around*. It was begun out of the stillness that authentic art requires. "What does this want to be?"

Art, from scraps. Art from what's already there. Art as rearrangement. There's nothing new. Ever. We see what would like to emerge next. And then next. I feel as if we're moving into a work of art, filled with the love of place, the love of conserving and appreciating. Our condo was one of the first to be occupied. The owner was able to scavenge an old claw-foot bathtub, some faucets, some hardware, and a fire door covered with embossed tin. It's very cool.

59   Me & Job

A LITTLE TALE: YOU look up. A small snowball loosens from the ledge above. Then another. Then an entire chunk of the ledge dislodges and pours downward. You move quickly across, but it's as if the mountain itself is headed for your lap. All you can do now is what you were taught, duck under, try to maintain an air-hole to the surface. And wait. People know where you are, so there's reason not to despair.

Ah, drama. You've heard all this before: Jerry and I had returned from a lovely trip to Michigan's Upper Peninsula when I was diagnosed with cancer. First cancer, then eye surgery, twice, then Jerry's back surgery, then the suspicion that there's plaque in his carotid arteries. Then I had hip pain. NOW I have shingles. I had the vaccine, but it only prevents about 50% of the cases. I do think of Job now and then, his unwillingness to curse God in response to all the terrible things God supposedly did to him. "Naked I came out of my mother's womb, and naked shall I return: the Lord has given, and Lord has taken away; blessed be the name of the Lord."

When Job protests that he's innocent of wrongdoing, God's only answer comes out of the whirlwind, "Where were you when I laid the foundations of the earth?"

I'm feeling pretty punk right now. Really down. That bears repeating. Really down. At such times, it seems built into us to look for a way out, an air-hole, rescue of some sort. There's always the "s---happens" response, the shrugged shoulders, but I don't believe that one for a minute. There's anger and despair in it. Then there's the

"What did I do wrong?" response. As if I were a nicer person, nothing bad would happen to me. Oh really? I won't get sick and die if I'm nice enough? If I'd taken care of myself better? I should never have thought about moving to a condo right now. It spiked my adrenalin and taxed my precious already-compromised immune system! And then there's the pit of depression, which, as we know, is anger covered over. More of the same "Why me? It's unfair!"

I look in the mirror. There's this gray-haired person with incredibly tight curls staring at me, with her neck wrinkles. Who is this stable "me" I've come to believe exists? An accumulation of memories.

When nothing's stable, there's still this fluctuating beauty, this raw energy of living. Says Job, in so many words. He says, "I don't know s— about why anything happens, but the happening itself is good." And there's God saying, "Right on. You don't know s—."

If you've had shingles, or know someone who has, you understand a little how I feel. I don't so much hurt, as is typical, but itch— fiercely, like the worst poison ivy I've ever had. The doctor told me to get Capsaicin cream, which is sold for arthritis, essentially a pain-killer by means of masking the discomfort with ground-up Jalapeno peppers. It works pretty well, but woe unto you if you get it on your fingers and at any time in the next 24 hours put your contacts in. I've tried all the tricks, washing my hands with vinegar, with milk. Nothing does much good.

It's also like having the flu. My glands are sore, I feel tired and sick. And of course ANY symptom of any sort enhances the ever-present awareness of my mortality that cancer has bequeathed me. Which reminds me: my first CT scan since the end of chemo is coming up in early March.

And, the snow and cold keep coming. I've loved it, but you can only have so much. People around here say this is like the old days. I think the old days were something you had to be born to, to appreciate.

Nonetheless, here I am, slogging away, writing, at least this. Poems—yes, I'm writing again. But not many. The poems are holding back, almost not wanting to be written, so few seeing the light of day. Can't explain any of this. Can't explain anything.

60   The Party Planner

So, I'm stuck at home with the dreaded shingles, while 14,000 of my dearest friends are having a party in Seattle. They're wining and dining and schmoozing and lobbying and jockeying and laughing. And wining and dining, did I say that? I have learned to love AWP (the Association of Writers and Writing Programs) and their annual convention. Well, sort of love. I always leave home saying, "Why Oh Why Am I Going?" and I come home saying, "Let me tell you what happened on Thursday! And about this amazing reading! Guess who I got to have breakfast with?"

I almost didn't believe that I'd be able to go, anyway. Frankly, I was scared of going, of seeing old friends the first time after cancer, not looking like myself. Not having my old energy. Maybe not up for it at all. I used to go to hear what's going on among writers, to avoid isolation and, as a sidelight, attend and/or be on a few panels. Part of that's still true. But these days I go almost entirely to see old friends.

Of course I hate AWP, too. Most writers I know are introverts like me. It's torture for us to stand in a loud room with a glass of wine and try to yell a trivial comment to the person desperately trying to think of what to say in return. At my age, many of the panels are about issues I've lost interest in a long time ago. But I'm happy when I can hear from someone I admire. This happens, too.

There are purists who wouldn't be caught dead at AWP. It's one of the largest, craziest conferences in the country. But consider: all these people are there because they write, because they're hungry for talk about writing, about how to be a better writer, how to promote writing in their communities. They want to hear some of the best writers in the country read their work. Not such ignominious reasons.

One way to be part of a community of writers is to stay home and read good books. Frankly, I think we'd all be better off if we did more of that and less schmoozing. But I've noticed that those who do go and schmooze are often also very well read and work like dogs to be good writers. This is one of their few "social" moments.

My grandmother used to say that I was born arranging a party. I don't at all think of myself that way, but then, I see me in Akron when I was six, setting up my little table in the front yard, making peanut butter sandwiches, cutting them into small pieces, and inviting the neighbor kid to my "party." He must have gone home to tell his mother about the party, because a bit later, there he was, all cleaned up, hair slicked down, dressed as I'd never seen him before.

There's a photo of my fifth birthday party at the lake, six children around the picnic table, me smiling like the queen. Me at my "bunking party" in seventh grade, making a silly face.

How to reconcile those versions of "me"? I've noticed that in a crowd, I can feel anonymous, yet part of things. I can stand back and kvell over the collection of family or friends, yet still be standing back in my mind a bit. Here I am, with my wine and napkin, glad everyone's there, but oops, I need some more cheese and crackers, excuse me for a moment.

Last winter, when I was in the middle of treatment and couldn't go, my Rainier Writing program friends called me to toast me. It was as good as being there. Almost.

61   The New Normal

WHAT IS THIS "GETTING over" cancer treatment? Or "getting over" anything, for that matter? We may go to therapy, we may meditate or "forgive," or whatever our practice calls for, but we don't shed the past like an old skin.

I went for my six-month post-treatment follow-up with my oncologist's nurse practitioner. (They're putting off a scan until closer to my one-year mark, in June.) I told her I feel a fair amount of fatigue, that I need a nap—often for an hour—every afternoon, and she said, "Well, that's your new normal."

Oh yeah? I thought.

According to Anne Katz, in her book, *After You Ring the Bell. . .10 Challenges for the Cancer Survivor*, one study found that 33% of cancer survivors report that they've had fatigue for a total of about two weeks in any one month, more than five years after treatment. So about half the time, people who've had chemo and/or radiation feel tired. As Katz says, the tiredness is not helped by rest or sleep and is "greater in magnitude and persists longer than would be expected with fatigue for any other reason, such as exercise."

Well, duh, you half-poison anything with chemicals—your body, the earth—and it shows the effects for a long, long time. Rippling effects. More vulnerability to other diseases, to more cancer, to osteoporosis, to more fatigue.

But Katz has a whole chapter on exercise with the clear message that the more you can do, the less you'll be tired. Well, duh again. I know that, but when you've felt bad for a long time, you develop a different attitude, that maybe you need to "take care" of yourself, get plenty of sleep. Rest. People say that to you because they can't think of anything else that might be helpful, and they want to help. You begin to believe it.

The farther I get from treatment, the more I see that I won't ever be the same. This is good to acknowledge, because instead of thinking any day now this will be better, I can begin to adjust. If I'd had a leg amputated, I'd finally say, "Okay, this is the way it is. Now let's see how much I can do with what I have."

So, what can I do? The winter's has been so very long and cold. It was below zero again this morning. My exercise routine has been way truncated. I've been walking—either at the Commons, where we'll be moving—or at the mall with Jerry for about a mile every day. Not good enough, I know, but about right for Jerry after his back surgery. I need to pick up the pace. What I really need is warm weather, and my bike.

I've spent a lot of hours in my life at a desk. Or sitting in a chair reading. But if you want to have energy, you have to use it. I can't believe the ridiculous simplicity of this. I can't believe I'm even having to talk about this. I, who have always loved to walk, swim, bike. The difference is, now it's serious. Do it or else.

That message, "Get used to it. This is the new normal," was good for me. I am not about to give in to this tiredness until I've proven there's no help for it. Hear me and Helen Reddy roar.

It is sobering, that one doesn't just return to "normal." I want to be the same person, full of optimism and energy. Yet there's that bass note, as I've called it before, of mortality.

I could now say what a good thing it is to grow wiser, etc. And all that's true! How strong the inclination is to balance the scales—one good thing for one bad thing! I'd rather look as squarely as I can into the lion's mouth, count the teeth, and say "So? My head's in the lion's mouth. Let's see, I may have time to write another book before he snaps his jaws. I may get to see my youngest grandchild graduate from college. The lion may grow tired and back off. Why waste my time trying to analyze the situation?"

62   Old Scarecrow

I'M HERE TO TELL you that recently *I survived three days of teaching high school.* I was thinking this might make a good movie title. Then I thought of all those people who get up every day and do that, who wouldn't think that's funny at all. I was one of them, from 1970-75. Why it was a big deal for me is that I was really nervous that I couldn't hold up to EVEN that, three days. And only three classes, from 10:30-2:30. Art classes.

The art teacher had written a grant to bring several kinds of artists to her classes to expose her students to professionals in these various forms. Her students are—what's the euphemism?—"underserved"? The district is huge, miles and miles of mid-Michigan territory, most kids from places that aren't even dots on the map. Some kids ride the bus *two hours* to get to school and two hours home. Think of the kindergartners or first graders! The teacher says they're tired by the time they get to school. These kids have no access to the wider world. So hurray for the teacher who's giving them as much as she can.

Which is why I said I'd do this. It scared me in several ways. I've felt so out of the real, working world. These last two years of dealing with the physical body, mine and Jerry's. There's an inward-turning that happens even against the will. Not narcissism, but, well, separation. And high school students have their own world, eons removed from mine. How could I *not* have Yeats' "Among School Children" in my head?

Better to smile on all that smile, and show
There is a comfortable kind of old scarecrow.

Then, too, could I simply hold up, considering that I seem to need a long nap every afternoon? The school where I taught is an hour away. So I had a long drive on the front and back end of the teaching day.

I did hold up (with a nap when I got home). It was good for me! I felt this inward energy come forth to meet the situation—fragments of the young high school teacher step up and behave like, well, a high school teacher. I was a pretty good one, actually. I taught at a large, consolidated school in Arkansas like this one, with children from rural, mostly uneducated backgrounds.

So, the same issues began in my head: what about these children— so, so many of them—who sleep though class, who are autistic, angry, abused, lethargic from poor nutrition? I imagined taking just one of the more alert ones out of there and whisking her away to a private school in the East like the one four of my grandchildren have attended, putting them among peers who are motivated, who have energy for learning because their homes are stable and encouraging.

It's the peers! The teacher I worked with is a good teacher. She tries hard. Students like her. They gather in her room at lunchtime, just because they like being there. But too many miss day after day, or sleep through class. They don't care about grades, many of them. (Yet she's evaluated on the progress her students make!) They don't motivate each other. Au contraire, they encourage each other in staring at their cellphones even when they're supposed to be put away. Few of them finished what I asked them to do. It makes me sad. I used to rant and rail, thinking I had some answers, if people would only listen. Now I don't know. I'm not sure I have answers. The only answer I have to anything these days is "Do what you can to help, day by day."

As I said, though, in a small way, taking on this little "job" flipped a switch in my head. Even if I have less energy, I feel more like my old self.

63   Literature Heaven

OLD ANTHOLOGIES, FOR INSTANCE, what can you do with them? We have dozens, all our years of Nortons, plus. It's humbling to see the shifts in great names, who's left out, who's given a large sampling. I've edited an anthology, myself. Does one go for breadth? Sheer quality? Diversity?

I'm re-living my academic and early writerly life. End of that chapter, start of another one. Oh well, writers are always starting over. Especially poets. With every blank page. But over our shoulders, there's still and always the presence of the writers we've modeled ourselves on. The *anthologized ones.*

Who "lasts"? Who decides? Screeds get written on this subject. Since I've come face-to-face with my mortality, those questions look different to me. Longer range. Young writers are scrambling for notice, and who can blame them? Who can blame any of us for wanting to be read? For wanting whatever our work is to be worth our lives?

How can my work be worth my entire creative life if in twenty years all my books are compost? How can my teaching be of any worth if most students can't remember one thing they read a year from now? Is a writing life only worth having if we keep showing up in anthologies? For that matter, is the life of a musician only worth it if the music is played a hundred years from now? All art, the same.

From here, at my age, I see the creative life as a vast human endeavor. Not single, not "famous," but everything together, each part feeding the rest. As in the Renaissance, gatherings of energy that fuel insights.

Insights get lost. Sure. A few people knew the world was round in the 6th century B.C., but it was hundreds of years before most believed it. What the Buddhists learned about human consciousness was lost to the Western world for 2,500 years and is only now being "discovered." Sometimes what's "known" is utterly wrong, but gradually a correction comes. Reality won't be denied.

Sorry for all my philosophizing as I pull out things I haven't looked at for years! This move feels like a major shift, more than any other move. Is it toward old age?—we're buying a condo, after all. Not quite that. I think it's a new sense (the product, maybe, of illness), both of the vital importance of what I do and the utter insignificance of it.

Even if I live a long life, there are maybe 20 years left of it. There's only one me. Every fiber of my being is crucial to the whole, as Walt Whitman would have said. I don't know how or why, but I feel that it is so. This *being* is walking every day, between 1 ½ and 2 miles, mostly indoors. It was zero degrees last night. Some days I think I'll die of claustrophobia. Where is my Wobbly Bicycle? In the shed. Pining away.

I've also made an appointment with an "Integrative medicine" physician, well-known locally for having cured, apparently, her husband of a cancer that all the doctors at the University of Michigan hospital and other places had given up on. She uses nutrition, vitamins and other non-traditional healing techniques. I need to see what she has to offer. I got shingles. Then I had an allergy attack. And I'm tired. I'll try anything as long as it doesn't hurt me.

Anthologies? That's where I began here. With what lasts, what doesn't. Nothing lasts. We act as if we don't know that. Since the body won't last, we hang onto a last-ditch hope of immortality.

The idea of heaven, maybe, or of our work, lasting through the ages.

But I think about the word *immortal*. Without mortality. Without death. The word doesn't imply that one doesn't die. It says "without death." "Deathless." Not having the quality of death. Everything dies, yet nothing dies. In some sense that's impossible to articulate, those who make art are surely as aware of that as our perpetually anthologized guy, Walt:

I have heard what the talkers were talking, the talk of the beginning and the end,
But I do not talk of the beginning or the end.

There was never any more inception than there is now,
Nor any more youth or age than there is now,
And will never be any more perfection than there is now,
Nor any more heaven or hell than there is now.

Urge and urge and urge,
Always the procreant urge of the world.

64   The Gift

"NOT I, NOT I, but the wind that blows through me." This is D. H. Lawrence.

In this country, where we irrationally hold to the belief that we're egalitarian, we don't like very much the definition of talent as a gift. We like to say anyone can muscle their way into accomplishing anything if only she tries hard enough. Which, it seems to me, affects our attitude toward the arts themselves.

What is a "gift"? I just got hold of Lewis Hyde's *The Gift: Creativity and the Artist in the Modern World*, written in the 70s and newly reissued. It's a gift. A deeply insightful look at what it means to give and receive a gift, particularly the gift of art/music/poetry.

"It is the assumption of this book that a work of art is a gift, not a commodity," Hyde says. "Or, to state the modern case with more precision, that works of art exist simultaneously in two "economies," a market economy and a gift economy. Only one of these is essential, however; a work of art can survive without the market, but where there is no gift, there is no art."

A gift is a thing we do not get by our own effort. This is Hyde's definition. How this works: In a market economy, it's tit-for-tat. I give you $5, you give me a product that's worth $5. We remain unconnected except for this transaction. If I need a $5 loan and you charge me 6% interest, there's even more distance between us. I am not part of your "tribe" at all. You can use me to make money. If you charge me unreasonable interest, it becomes usury, which is a downright hostile arrangement.

As long as things are tit-for-tat, there's no motion. Anything contained within its own boundary dies of exhaustion eventually. But when you give a gift, there is momentum, and the weight shifts from body to body.

If I give a gift, you may or may not give me something later. If you do, your gift may or may not be equal to what I gave you. There's a gap, a mystery. This Something between us holds us together in an inarticulate way. I wait, and the waiting is a trust and a forward momentum; I can have no idea where it's going. If you refuse my gift, it has no value. It's the passage of the gift that matters. Thomas Merton said that the begging bowl of the Buddha "represents the ultimate theological root of the belief, not just in a right to beg, but in openness to the gifts of all beings as an expression of the interdependence of all beings."

A gift must be constantly consumed, passed from one to the next. It is a live thing. It seeks the barren, the arid, the stuck, and the poor. The gifts that were sent to me last year when I was in chemo and radiation were literally reservoirs of available life—"Here, this is my vitality, my life energy, that I package up and send to you."

But get this! The value, the increase of the gift comes, not in the first transaction, but when the gift is then passed on again, when it moves from second to third party. When gratitude enters the movement. When it has passed *through* somebody. Through me. I'm using it right now, I hope. Passing it on the best I can.

The transformation is not accomplished until we have the power to give the gift *on our own terms.*

Hyde says, "A gifted artist contains the vitality of his gift within the work, and thereby makes it available to others." What about when the artist charges for it? That's fine, if it's for support. That doesn't destroy the gift's nature. It's when something remains behind as profit that the gift begins to die.

It may look as if artists are lazy people who ought to be supporting themselves. I think how fortunate I was all those years to have the patronage of a university, a public institution that said to me, "We want you to teach, but we also want you to do your art, and we'll give you time and pay to do both." But not everyone is lucky that way. This is where the issue becomes political. Where we start thinking about the National Endowment for the Arts and other such programs. Here's my picture of, say, our country: If everything is cash nexus, there is only the spinning wheel of commerce that goes nowhere but around and around. It's not necessarily evil, but it alone leaves the spirit—the national spirit—cold, unnurtured.

The old lover's quarrel between liberty and community, as Hyde puts it. Westerners defend freedom and long for attachment.

But the gifts—for example, the artist whose whole passionate life is contained in her work—create a momentum, that gap of giving that leaves an uncertainty. It's uncertainty, unbalance, that creates motion. I give you this poem. What will happen next? If you read it, it may change you in some way, you may pass it on to another reader. I don't know what will happen and I don't know what my gift is "worth," or what it may amount to later.

The writers I know, including me, feel uncertain all the time. Will you want to read this book? Is it any good? I'm sure that uncertainty is necessary. We know we have to stay out of the marketplace to some extent. The gift is fragile, uncontrollable. It can get steamrollered by commerce. Even by the politics we support and work toward. We have to be careful with it. And then we have to do the work and fling it into the atmosphere, not knowing if or when it will land.

65   Sinking into the Soil

SOME PLACES REACH INTO your gut and take hold. Others not. I'm thinking a lot about place, of course, since we're almost finished packing and on May 1 we'll be moving. Until we retired in 2007, I'd never lived in Michigan. Yet it's always been my home. You'd think I would have adopted Delaware, being their poet laureate and all. Raising my children for half their lives there. It's a lovely state in so many ways, but I never properly sank into its soil.

I learned to walk close to the shore of our lake just north of here. Northern Michigan has been my spiritual home. I could say a lot more—but we have to fill these moving boxes.

And we needed to pause to visit my father in Missouri for his 96th birthday. He could have come to live near us. Near family. But he's lived in Missouri the better part of his life, and his lady friend (yes) lives in the same complex where he has an independent living cottage. His family—his grandsons and granddaughter, his daughters and sons-in-law—all drove and flew in to be with him. He of course kept mentioning the cost, how crazy of us to spend the money. Still, he was smiling his shy smile. This is the first time he's seen me since the cancer. When we talked on the phone, he says, "Boy I sure hope the cancer doesn't come back." Or, I guess you have a chance of living through this." Or, "I guess you don't have any hair." Stuff like that, to cheer me up. When he saw me he didn't register, as far as I could tell, the dramatic difference in my hair. I mentioned it to him. He said, "Well, I guess it's curlier." Not much interested in such things.

Every phone call all winter during my treatment, I'd just say, "Well, I don't feel so great right now, but in a few days I'll feel better." Always the upbeat.

66   It's All Lending

I'M LOOKING OUT THE window in front of my desk through the trees at two of the unrestored buildings on the grounds of the old mental hospital, a rotting tower on one, a turret on another. We're almost flying up here, with our 14 windows. Sun is pouring into the one on my left, and if I look hard, I can imagine I see a thin line of the bay between the trees and Old Mission peninsula.

It is all so ELEGANT. These high old windows, thick plaster walls, expansive wood floors. It's an adjustment from our cute little bungalow on 8th Street. By the time we left—5 days ago!—we'd made it really pretty. Wally would rather be there. He scolded and fussed at us all the first night here. Let's go home! Ceilings are too high here! Not enough crevices and dark places. A wide hallway out there I'm not allowed in! But he likes his new cat tree and is settling in. Whither thou goest.

This is the first moment I've had to sit and collect myself. That's an interesting expression, isn't it? I was "scattered," and now I pull myself back into a group of concepts I recognize.

I wonder if this new place itself will shift what or how I write. As if there were a "way." Still, I think of Emily Dickinson in her father's old house, at her small writing desk, her small scraps of paper, her poems dense as flourless cake. I think of Georgia O'Keeffe, her huge desert paintings, broad expanses of color. (Of course her flowers are like that, too, and she didn't paint most of them in the desert. The mind is its own expanse, which, I guess, contradicts my original thought.)

We write about our landscape, but that's not the same as what the landscape does to us, as we feel its presence within our articulation. I wish to change that word, "landscape" to "ground." "Landscape" feels like observation of a scene. By "ground" I mean what we can't escape, the whole of it, as in The Ground of our Being.

It's good to have this radical change. To imagine leaving behind cancer, the year of chemo and radiation, the fear. And last winter's back surgery for Jerry. Yet the oncologist's office just called to say they've set up my CT scan for early June, in preparation for my one-year checkup in mid-June. I get a chilly spine, the chill that will always be there, that will never go away, but often is drowned out—by packing to move, for example, and arranging things in this gorgeous new place.

I guess carrying with me a heightened awareness of death is perhaps the only benefit of having cancer. The awareness of death permeates all joy just as the awareness of joy permeates all grief. It wouldn't be called grief otherwise, right? All the pixels are there, inseparable, the dark and the light.

We're unpacked, a quiet is beginning to reign, although our paintings are leaning against the walls waiting for our guy who can drill into plaster and not crack it to pieces. Our bookcases will be installed on Monday and we can begin unboxing the books and arranging them all over again. Our "Estate Sale" is tomorrow and Saturday at our old house. Lending. It's all lending. We use things for years. We let them go. Someone else uses them. Our old mattress is leaning against the fence in the alley waiting for the American Waste people to haul it away, for it to begin to break into its component parts, to shift however slowly into another life.

Postscript

I WILL NOT SNEER at Facebook any more. There are at this point 252 "likes" since I reported that my one-year scan had come back clean. I read all the comments. Uncharacteristically for me, I went through the entire list of "likes," slowly picturing the people I know, or barely know, and imagining the ones I didn't. They checked "like." How do they know of me? Not important. Important is the heightened awareness the "likes" give me of our community of humans who wish each other well. Who've wished me well. Whoops, there's another as I write. 253. And comments: one says: "Grinning." I'm grinning. It's not nothing. It's not trivial.

I had no idea that an all-clear signal from my oncologist would rattle my innards so profoundly. It doesn't mean much—he said so. But for me, it set off a series of adjustments as if I had just crawled out from under the rubble of a bombed-out building. I'd been down there a long time in the dark—dirt, sand, creaking timbers—injured, starving and thirsty. I'd nearly died. Now what? Can I ever go back to who I was? Who I thought I was? What now?

No joke. That big a shift. Take the metaphor of my hair. Take my hair. It's too curly for me. Well, of course I'm grateful to have it. It sprang back from the brutal treatment with great vivacity, all thick and, well, curly. I feel as if my grandmother had just coerced me up the block to have the dreaded perm.

And then who is the person who has to have long naps, Wally stretched across her stomach? Who's losing her lithe young body? Who can't get her stomach flat no matter how smart she eats? Some days I'm just plain depressed. I was brave. Now what got pushed aside by the bravery wants to be seen.

Don't misunderstand me. Some days I'm fine.

And then the writing. I don't know. The fire, where's the fire? Some of it used to come from the need to succeed. Sure. Some from my previous publish-or-perish life. Sure. Some. For the past couple of years I've had to force myself to get things ready to send out. I have a pile of unsent poems. I'm a bit floundering. I can't figure out how to relate to my life. I'm a bloodhound who hasn't picked up the scent. You could say I'm waiting to pick it up, to figure this out. Or, you could say that all that previous "figuring out" was not the point. There's nothing to figure out. I lean toward the latter. What comes next will come next.

Post-post script

I DID MAKE THE trip to Tacoma this year for the Rainer residency!

Then it was time to return home. I was supposed to meet the van for the airport at 3:45 a.m. I heard a knock, thought it might be something upstairs above me, checked the peep-hole and saw nothing, went back to bed. A few minutes later, a fierce pounding on the door. This time I opened it. There was Kent, my colleague, frantic. "Fleda, the van is here! You were supposed to be down-stairs 15 minutes ago!" Watch me throw on my clothes. Watch me sweep my things into my bag. Watch me stumble to the van, wild hair, no makeup, belt in my hand.

I'd mis-set my clock.

Chemo-brain, I guess. Stuff like that is more likely for me these days. And I often can't remember the simplest, more familiar, names of people and things.

At the residency, we had a guest, a poet and editor of a well-known journal, who also happens to be a radiation oncologist. [Side note: I mentioned this to my chiropractor, who said, "Oh, poetry must be a good way for him to let off some tension from his job." Sigh. Poetry as nice, innocent stress-reliever.]

Back to the story. This poet/editor/physician was talking about the origin and effects of Taxol, one of the chemo drugs I was given. Taxol was developed from the yew tree. Before someone figured out how to make it from the cells of the needles, it took the bark of a whole tree to make enough drug for one patient. The huge benefit of Taxol and Carboplatin (I had both), both from the same source, is that they work better and have fewer side effects than the old drugs. They aren't as potent, but they hang onto the cells longer. Hence, as he told me later, in his experience, one side-effect, fatigue, is likely to persist for a long while. Sometimes two years.

Why is it that he knows this and told me this and all my oncology nurse said to me about my fatigue is "Get used to it. This is your new normal." Maybe she thought so. But still.

I was nervous about going to Tacoma to teach for ten whole days. Could I hold up? The director did what he could to help me, spaced out my work load leaving time for a nap every day. I paced myself. Sometimes got tired, but then so did everyone else. But I have to say that ten days of residency did more for my spirit than anything has, since the end of chemo. Ten days with my dear wonderful, fiercely-good writing friends. Laughing. Good lord, every day something hilarious. And all the rest. My teaching gears were so glad to be engaged—they cranked up, rattled away the rust, and took off.

I also saw, while I was there, how I'm changed. I think it's harder to see that, close to home. There's a separation, a sense of the quick passing of things, of everyone's quick passing. Not in a gloomy way, but in a way that makes me love us, all of us, tenderly. A tenderness. That's what I think I want to say. A happiness that's not concerned with the quick passing of things.

Best thing anyone said to me while I was there: my former student Katy saw me for the first time and impulsively said, just before hugging me, "Oh, THANK you for living!"

So, that's the gist of it. I'm living. I've been living all along, but it seems as if my cells are perking up, little by little, shedding their trauma as much as they can, the best they can. I'm at last getting some good writing done. Going back to poems I wrote last year, combing their hair, applying some lipstick, getting them ready to travel out of here.

Notes

THERE ARE MANY BOOKS mentioned in these entries. I have only noted the ones I've directly quoted from or have talked about at some length. These are listed in order of appearance:

Susan Sontag, *Illness as Metaphor,* (Farrar, Straus, & Giroux, 1978).

Ted Kooser, "Feb. 21, Sunny and Clear," from *Winter Morning Walks,* (Pittsburgh: Carnegie Mellon University Press, 2000.), p. 98.

Fleda Brown and Sydney Lea, *Growing Old in Poetry: Two Poets, Two Lives,* (Autumn House Press, e-edition, 2012).

Robert Louis Stevenson, "Land of Counterpane," from *A Child's Garden of Verses,* 1885.

Ray Bradbury, from a Nov. 1979 review of a book about the National Air and Space Museum in Washington, D.C.

Ann Carson, "The Glass Essay," from *Glass, Irony, and God,* (New Directions Press), p. 37

Muriel Barbery, *Elegance of the Hedgehog,* (Penguin, 2002).

Interview with Christian Wiman, *Image Magazine,* Issue 76.

Christian Wiman, *My Bright Abyss: The Meditations of a Believer,* (New York: Farrar, Straus and Giroux, 2013), P. 111.

Sokuzan Bob Brown, a dharma transmitted Soto Zen Priest and my teacher, made the brush and ink drawing that begins Chapter 27.

Steve Hagen, *Buddhism: Plain and Simple,* (New York: Broadway Books, 1997), p. 42.

Elinor Wilner, "Cold Dawn of the Day When Bush Was Elected For a Second Term," is from *Tourist in Hell*, (Chicago: University of Chicago Press, 2010).

Stephen Greenblatt, *The Swerve: How the World Became Modern*, (New York: W. W. Norton, 2011), 196.

Debra Bruce, "Ariel View," from *Survivor's Picnic*, (Word Tech Press, 2012).

Ann Pancake, "Creative Responses to Worlds Unraveling: The Artist in the 21st Century," *The Georgia Review*, (Fall 2013) 412–413.

Maxim Gorky, *A Childhood: An English Translation*, (Government Institutes), 2010, p. 143.

Paul Johnson, *Mozart: A Life*. (Penguin, 2013).

Jerry Dennis, *The Windward Shore* (Ann Arbor: The University of Michigan Press 2011), p. 118.

Doris Grumbach, *Fifty Days of Solitude*, (Beacon Press: Boston, 1994), p. 33.

Anne Katz, *After You Ring the Bell. . .10 Challenges for the Cancer Survivor* (Oncology Nursing Society, 2011).

D. H. Lawrence, "Song of the Man Who Has Come Through"

Lewis Hyde, *The Gift: Creativity and the Artist in the Modern World*, (New York: Vintage   Books, 1979), p. xvi.